THE DANCING LEAF

THE DANCING LEAF

Embracing the Timeless Wisdom of Tao Te Ching

SURBHI KAKAR

HAY HOUSE INDIA

New Delhi • London • Sydney

Carlsbad, California • New York City

Hay House Publishers (India) Pvt. Ltd.
Muskaan Complex, Plot No.3, B-2 Vasant Kunj, New Delhi-110 070, India
Hay House Inc., PO Box 5100, Carlsbad, CA 92018-5100, USA
Hay House UK, Ltd., The Sixth Floor, Watson House, 54 Baker Street, W1U 7BU, UK
Hay House Australia Pty Ltd., 18/36 Ralph St., Alexandria NSW 2015, Australia

Email: contact@hayhouse.co.in
www.hayhouse.co.in

This book does not promote or favour any religion or practice. The intent of the author is only to offer information of a general nature to help you in your quest for emotional, physical, and spiritual well-being.

ISBN 978-93-94613-95-9
ISBN 978-93-94613-89-8 (ebook)

Printed at Repro India Limited

To the creative life force which flows through
everything in this universe.
Thank you for writing this work through me.

Contents

Foreword

The Dancing Leaf is a book on self-culture written by Ms Surbhi Kakar who is an Indian data scientist based in the Netherlands. It is a free, short, and appreciative commentary on the great Chinese book Tao Te Ching, which is one of the most translated texts in world literature. The reputed author of the book, Lao Tzu, is considered to be a semi-legendary figure and a deity in religious Taoism and traditional Chinese religions. Yet, the personal life of this enigmatic philosopher-saint is shrouded in mystery.

The story goes that after being disillusioned by his inability to transform society into his ideal way of life, he decided to move away from his country. While travelling on the back of a buffalo, he came across the western gate of the city where he was recognised by the gateman who persuaded him to at least jot down his teaching and leave it as a parting gift to civilisation. This he did and the product was a slim volume of 81 verses called Tao Te Ching. It roughly translates to *The Way and Its Power.* Ms Surbhi has preferred to call it *The Book of the Way and of Virtue.*

Tao Te Ching is the bible of Taoism (also pronounced Daoism), the mystical philosophy of China. The central concept of the book is the path of moral behaviour in accordance with the absolute Tao. What is the Tao? It is hard to define. Apparently, it is the course of nature, but for the followers of Taoism, it is the ultimate reality, something like the impersonal Brahman of the Upanishads. Tao Te Ching teaches a kind of quiet mysticism, a 'do nothingness' or 'a creative quietude'. It advocates filling life with a tranquil spontaneity and having silent obedience to what life has ordained for an individual. It inspires us to restore peace and harmony that is destroyed by our foolish rush for worldly success. Using many similes, the book tries to guide the followers to a peaceful and completely self-collected state of mind comparable to yogic samadhi. The followers are advised to adhere to the life force that sustains them; they have to stop thrashing and flailing around and trust nature to buoy and carry them gently forward, like water does. In fact, water is the closest parallel to Tao in the natural world because of its resilience, flexibility, adaptability, shapelessness, calm resignation to situations, etc. And by imbibing the infinite suppleness of water and its incomparable inner strength, people would then be able to act without strain, persuade without argument, make their point without violence, be eloquent without a flourish, etc.

The title, *The Dancing Leaf,* meaningfully conjures up our life's journey vis-à-vis the journey of a leaf. When the leaf falls off the tree, says Ms Surbhi, it lets go of all its attachment to the tree and allows the wind to take it anywhere. It dances and enjoys the process of returning to where it belonged. The book invites the readers to live this journey of the dancing leaf and enjoy the effortlessness of life.

This book is especially useful for contemporary people obsessed with physical fitness. Fitness should mean a healthy mind in a healthy body. The role of the mind in our lives is enormous. Bodily fitness can only be of significance if it is accompanied by mental fitness. With determination, a person with a sick body can still do wonderful things; you know Gorky was very sick, and so were Kafka, Dostoevsky, and Nietzsche. The great physicist Stephen Hawking was virtually a wheelchair-borne brain. Therefore, mental health is so important for a happy and successful life. And the main aim of *The Dancing Leaf* is to help readers reengineer their mental world, their personal lives, their personalities, priorities, aims, ambitions, and goals so that the inner calm is not lost which is of vital importance. Her objective is to enable readers to slow down and listen to themselves, face the difficult questions of everyday life and create a harmony between the life within and the cosmos without.

The book also has a rare accessibility and relatability which is sure to connect well with the reader. The 'Take Aways' section gives in a nutshell what has been covered in a particular chapter and how readers can immediately put it to use in life. Another salient feature of the book is its appeal to reason and eschew dogmatism in any form so much so that religion hardly figures in it. But it has a liberal dose of spiritualism, mysticism, and the higher religion that unites mankind. In a sense, we can say that the book belongs to the genre of applied psychology and applied ethics. It is a manual of self-culture with an emphasis on the application, practice, and use of our inner wisdom through self-enquiry.

Effortless Action, Being Nothing, Being Water, Attachment to Completion, and The Bliss of Letting Go of Bliss are some of the titles of the twenty-four chapters that make *The Dancing Leaf*. Every chapter is important and filled with enlightening and eye-opening insights.

Surbhi has packed the book with personal experiences too. She has chronicled how she has benefited from the eternal wisdom available in the Tao Te Ching, Upanishads, Gita, Yogasutra, and many other profound books.

The readers should go slow with this book, savour it, and let the wisdom in it sink into them. This way, they are sure to experience inner transformation and reap priceless and rewarding benefits.

I compliment Surbhi Kakar for having produced such an edifying and much-required book. I also hope that the book gets wide publicity and attracts readers' attention and love.

—Dr Sibnath Sarma

Retired professor of philosophy,

Gauhati University, India

Introduction

Sometime back, I moved from my home country (India) to another country with my husband. At the time, I did not realise how big a change this was going to be for me and for my life. I had been doing my spiritual practices before this and had full confidence that I could go beyond any obstacle that life presented me with.

However, after shifting, in my journey of connecting with and living my authentic self every moment (which I call living a life of transformation), I began experiencing varying states. I found myself fluctuating between being happy, peaceful, blissful, loving, and allowing, and being angry, frustrated, struggling, confused, and resisting. I associated with some of these states (or you could also call them emotions) and separated myself from the others. However, I could see a missing piece in my practices and could not figure out what it was until I made the decision to move to a new country. This missing piece revealed itself to me through the teachings of Lao Tzu in the book Tao Te Ching.

Tao Te Ching is a very old Chinese text, dating back to the 4th century BC. This book has been perceived as a religious as well as a philosophical text. The authorship of this book is debatable, but most say it has been written by a sage named Laozi/Lao Tzu. The title of the book can be translated as *The Book of the Way and of Virtue.* But personally for me, this book refers to the way of my life, the journey of my life, and how I can live this journey in harmony.

I started reading the Tao Te Ching at a time when I was dealing with several breakdowns in my life. Later, I realised that I was going through a turmoil of emotions which were driven by guilt, self-doubt, and fear. The guilt of leaving my parents and parents-in-law behind led me to believe that I wasn't a good daughter and daughter-in-law. The self-doubt and fear arose from being in an unknown place and grappling with the new ways of life on both personal and professional levels. But the core truth was that starting a completely new life from scratch made me feel like I had lost my identity. And due to this, I always felt that I was on shaky ground that could collapse at any moment.

In such a space, I wasn't able to live fully in the present moment which meant that I was compromising on the clarity of my mind, self-expression, and inner confidence. All the spiritual practices that I earlier did somehow felt like a lot of hard work for me and did not come to me naturally. I became overcritical about doing the spiritual practices 'correctly'. Basically, I was trying to control the flow of life which resulted in a lot of struggle and disappointments. This was when Tao reached out to me to teach me the act of allowing. I realised that I had to learn how to allow life to flow in the way it is flowing.

It took some time to understand what I was dealing with and cultivate compassion for myself, and Tao helped me with this process.

I believe I stumbled upon Tao Te Ching through Dr Wayne Dyer. Dr Wayne Dyer is an established self-help author with a number of best-selling books. In one of his talks, I heard him speaking about this book and recommended trying out the practices given in it. This prompting inspired me to read the eighty-one verses of the Tao Te Ching. And as I was reading, I started documenting my experiences and created practices for myself. Soon, a desire showed up in me to share this work with everyone in the world. And this was the impetus that led to the inception of this book.

Every chapter in the book shares how I have implemented the verses in my life, the profound experiences I had during my practices, and how readers can achieve a similar transformational result. Through this book, I request the readers to consider the ideas I have expressed and experiment with them in their own lives by using the practices that I have designed.

Throughout the book, phrases like 'life of transformation', 'living an authentic life', and 'living a life of connecting back to self' have been used. This specifically refers to a life where one is committed to living in an empowered way by going beyond default limitations of mind and creating love and joy for everyone. Other expressions like 'higher self', 'inner being', and 'inner self' are also mentioned in the book in various places. This refers to that intelligent part of the self which is timeless and abundantly wise. Profound works such as

I Am That by Nisargadatta Maharaj and Sri Aurobindo's *Life Divine* mention the self as that part of us which is always constant, unchanging, and divine.

My intention behind writing this book

My primary objective is to ignite a spark of self-awareness in everyone's life through this book. In other words, this is an invitation for people to slow down and listen to themselves, face the difficult questions that show up every day in our lives, and create harmony within and without.

Why should someone read this book?

A lot of people find it difficult to read and take on practices given in the ancient texts. Through the experiences shared in the book, I believe that readers would be able to connect, contemplate, and implement the insightful teachings of Tao Te Ching in their own lives. This, in turn, would allow them to deal with day-to-day life issues and challenges which eat away at our fulfilment and self-expression. The ideas and practices given in the book when implemented can open up a new world where you see things differently and where there is ease, humility, and oneness between all beings.

I also strongly feel that this book has been written by the universe through me and I have very little to do with it.

How to use this book?

My request to you, dear reader, is to contemplate and consider the things you will read in this book. If you feel that it makes a difference to your life, then only take it else leave it. You are free to do what you resonate with. I also request you to be kind to yourself when practising these verses in your own life and not get stuck in the loop of 'I should do it all' or 'I should do it perfectly'.

Finally, I want to say that I am so proud of each one of you for just picking up this book and attempting to take this step on your journey of transformation. This act in itself shows how deeply committed you are to returning back to your true self. I am also deeply honoured by the trust you have bestowed on me as your guide on this path of self-enquiry and self-realisation.

The title of the book

When a leaf falls from a tree, it lets go of all its attachment to the tree and allows the wind to take it anywhere. The title of the book, *The Dancing Leaf*, signifies this way of life and encourages everyone to dance and enjoy this process of returning back to where they belong. All in all, my wish is that you find the ease and effortlessness of a dancing leaf after completing this book.

Take aways and how to practise sections

The 'Take Aways' section encapsulates the key ideas discussed in the chapter. It does so by expressing the ideas through different perspectives and examples. This section also consists of the wisdom shared by other spiritual masters around the ideas discussed in the chapter. All in all, the readers can see this section as a concise synopsis of all the important teachings and themes in the chapter.

You will also find the 'How to Practise' section in each chapter which would provide details regarding how you can adopt and implement the various teachings given in the book in a practical and easy manner.

For all the practices provided in this book, it would be best to maintain a journal. This can be an online journal or even a simple notebook which you can use as a journal. Documenting and journaling will not only give structure to your practice but also help in monitoring and tracking your progress. Therefore, I strongly recommend it.

For each entry, you can include the following details:

1. The practice you are taking up
2. The date when you took up a practice
3. Insights that arise on practising the exercises
4. Your observations or any experiences doing the same

However, you don't have to follow this if you don't resonate with it. If you are a person who feels like creating your own structure, that is also okay. The main goal is to allow yourself to touch the depths of your inner wisdom through self-enquiry and create the life of your choosing.

Chapter 1

Effortless Action

Yes, the words effortless and action sound a little contrasting. For us, an action means to do something or in more technical terms, to cause a change in a state. But have you considered that a non-action can also be an action?

We all have experienced this phenomenon in our lives when even without doing anything, the desired result was accomplished. This way of effortless living and effortless action can be found over and over again in several of Tao Te Ching's verses. For example, the second verse quotes:

> Realising this, the saint performs effortlessly according to the natural way without personal desire, and practices the wordless teaching through one's deeds.

Also, the tenth verse of the Tao Te Ching mentions:

> Can one gain the insight of nature and become a wise person without the effort of action?

For a major part of my life, I have been a hard worker. I have been taught since childhood that nothing can ever happen if you don't work hard for it. Therefore, all my life I worked hard to get good scores in my exams, to achieve professional growth, and to look good and be liked by people. I worked hard in almost all spheres of my life, even where working that hard wasn't required. The reason for this was that there was no way to know where to work hard and where not to and whether to work hard at all or not.

All of this undue pressure to do something in order to take charge of my life and steer it in a more advantageous direction led me to develop several unhealthy patterns. One of the patterns I developed was to victimise myself to come across as afraid and weak to people around me. The reason behind this was that nobody ever says anything to someone who is afraid and weak. But what I failed to realise was that I was trading my self-confidence for the sympathy of the people.

Another pattern that I had developed was to be constantly nice to people, even if it meant that I had to stifle my real emotions and never speak my mind. Again, the idea was the same: to remain in everyone's good books. After all, nobody messes with a person who is nice to everyone.

But when I started the transformation journey, it hit me what I had been doing throughout my life. I started getting conscious about everything and every action I was taking in my life, looking deeply at what was the cause behind all these actions. And once I realised the context behind my actions, I could alter it and change my actions accordingly.

For me, living a transformed life meant not operating from my default state. Whenever I got into a conflict with my family or at work, transformation for me meant to stop and create something empowering with these people. To stand in a place where I could create love with each of these people rather than re-acting on my past events in the present moment of time. This shift brought me closer to all of my relationships and I started experiencing fulfilment in these areas.

However, when I did not choose to be loved or when anything uncomfortable came up in these relationships again, without realising it, I started working hard to keep these relationships intact. The fact was that I got really attached to these relationships and wanted them to work at any cost. And the effort to maintain these relationships started to take a toll on me and I started experiencing fatigue and tiredness in my body. Yet despite all my efforts, there was a constant lack of harmony in my relationships, and I could not understand the reason for it. 'What was it that I was doing wrong?' I constantly asked myself.

It was when I started reading Tao Te Ching that I got an insight into what was actually going on. I realised that I was working too hard to make all my relationships work and constantly putting myself under stress whenever anything went wrong. But the greater insight was that through my actions, I wasn't just trying to influence my relationships; in actuality, I was trying to control life! And this attempt to create love and idealistic relationships wasn't only strenuous but also futile. Realising this, I started practising the art of non-action or effortless action.

Eventually, instead of instantly jumping into action and trying to force harmony during conflicts, I just chose to let things play out naturally. This didn't mean that I became indifferent and uninvolved, instead, it was more about disassociating from the situation and reflecting mindfully on what can I bring forth in my relationships. And when I stopped putting too much effort and instead embraced the effortless path, I was able to tackle problems and challenges in my relationships more effectively. This also removed the urge in me to take immediate action to fix everything which, in turn, freed me from the burden of constantly stressing and overworking myself.

The important point to note here is that it is never the task that creates struggle; it is the resistance to avoid a consequence or the compulsion to get a result which creates struggle. And only when we let go of our compulsions and resistances can we complete the task at hand in the most natural and effortless manner. This happens because, in the absence of forceful action, the universal energy can freely flow through us and guide us through the perfect way to execute a task. Simply put, if you allow it, the universe will work through you. The Bhagavad Gita captures the same essence when it says:

> For one who is happy in the Self alone, who is satisfied in the Self, who is content only in the Self, there is nothing that has to be done. [3:17]

Thus, we all should learn from rivers which flow effortlessly without putting in any hard work and eventually reach their destination. And when we stop struggling and working too hard to reach our goals, we will see that our desired results will reach out to us.

Take Aways

Our lives can be compared to the waves of the ocean. And just like the rise and fall of waves, when an unpleasant situation or emotion arises in us, it will eventually dissolve in some time. So, when everything is coming and going, rising and falling, like the waves of the ocean, why are you trying so hard to alter the flow of these waves? Trying to get rid of these uncomfortable emotions and fix everything in your life is like trying to alter the flow of these waves. Don't you think such an effort is futile? If you would just allow the wave to pass through, it would soon disappear in the vast ocean of your self. So, starting today, every time you have an urge to suddenly take an action in order to fix something, try to sit back and relax.

And if you are in doubt whether or not you will know about an uncomfortable thing or a situation that you need to get rid of, the answer is that you will know. Your inner being always knows when you want to get rid of something uncomfortable in your life. That's when no-action is required. This does not mean that you stop taking actions in your life in terms of your work, school, or at home. Instead, it just means allowing results to reach you without doing hard work for everything in your life!

How to Practise the Effortless Action

1. An integral part of effortless action is to inquire about the purpose and goal of our every action. So, before you undertake any task, stop for a moment and ask yourself:

    - What is it that I actually want?
    - Why is this action/task so important for me?
    - Will my action lead to any kind of genuine improvement or is it only for temporary satisfaction?
    - What will happen if I don't take action right now?

    By asking yourself such questions, you will notice that most of our actions are redundant and detrimental.

    Hence, before going ahead with any action, make sure to think about it from all perspectives and with a clear and composed mind.

2. Take some time out to observe the nature around you . . . birds, trees, rivers, sky, etc. Notice how it does all of its tasks effortlessly and only does what it is supposed to do without any attachment to any result. Hence,

we should take inspiration from nature in order to learn and properly implement the art of effortless action.

Chapter 2

BEING NOTHING

Whenever we say or use the word 'nothing', it usually denotes no-thing or the absence of everything. But if I ask you what 'being nothing' means, then what would you say? Does it mean not being anything? Or does it imply an absence of being? Or does it mean a being who has no features?

For me personally, the word 'nothing' implies an empty space and therefore, 'being nothing' means being an empty space. According to the Big Bang Theory, everything you see in this physical world emerged from empty space or nothingness. This means, you, I, and every living and non-living thing, or in other words, the whole cosmos came from this empty space. But how is it possible that an empty space can yield so much? It is only possible if what we consider as empty space or void is not empty at all. In fact, it is omnipotent and all-encompassing.

The first time I came across this hypothesis, it blew my mind, and it still amazes me every time I think about it. The world-renowned theoretical physicist, Professor Stephen Hawking, gave the following explanation of this theory:

> 'You enter a world where conjuring something out of nothing is possible. That is because at this scale, particles such as protons, behave according to the laws of nature we call "quantum mechanics", and they really can appear at random, stick around for a while, and then vanish again to reappear somewhere else.'

Thus, we can see that conjuring something out of nothing is possible. Another significant point to note here is that this empty space can be seen as something constant as this space is always there and it is only the particles that appear and disappear in this space.

Now if you imagine yourself as an empty space, i.e., a being that is beyond your body, then your thoughts, emotions, and judgements can be seen as analogous to the particles that appear and disappear at random. And in the way that empty space is omnipresent, so if you see yourself as an empty space, then you too are all-encompassing and constant.

Mesmerised and intrigued by this concept, I wanted to live my life being no-thing or as an empty space. A space which has nothing and still has the capacity to bear everything. But to my surprise, I found the same ideas being echoed in Tao Te Ching, which was written thousands of centuries ago.

The first verse of the Tao quotes:

> Tao (The Way) that can be spoken of is not the Constant Tao.
> The name that can be named is not a Constant Name.
> Nameless, is the origin of Heaven and Earth;
> The named is the Mother of all things.
> Thus, the constant void enables one to observe the true essence.
> The constant being enables one to see the outward manifestations.
> These two come paired from the same origin.
> But when the essence is manifested,
> It has a different name.
> This same origin is called 'The Profound Mystery'.
> As profound the mystery as It can be,
> It is the Gate to the essence of all life.

The eleventh verse of the Tao also mentions:

> Thirty spokes unite around one hub to make a wheel.
> It is the presence of the empty space that gives the function of a vehicle.
> Clay is moulded into a vessel. It is the empty space that gives the function of a vessel.
> Doors and windows are chisel out to make a room.
> It is the empty space in the room that gives its function.

> Therefore, something substantial can be beneficial.
> While the emptiness of void is what can be utilised.

While contemplating these verses, I got a revelation that silence is something very close to nothingness. Just as empty space implies no-thing, silence implies no-sound. Therefore, I started listening to silence. And if you carefully listen and focus on silence, you will find that this sound of silence is always there!

One thing I would like to mention here is that it takes consistent effort and determination to get accustomed and truly observe silence. Initially, it was difficult for me as well as I was constantly distracted by thoughts and the chatter in my mind. But I continued to be with all of it and started meditating for longer periods of time. And whenever my focus shifted, I gently moved it back to the sound of silence. And then one day, I had a vision; I saw the big bang and the entire evolution of the universe. In that moment, I experienced myself as a timeless and immortal being. I could see myself as a no-thing . . . as an empty space which had the entire universe within it!

This insight helped me improve my communication with people significantly. I realised that just like a vast, empty sky is not affected by grey clouds, similarly, if we become an empty space, clouds of judgements, biases, and expectations won't affect us. Such emotions are temporary and can never disturb the stillness of the sky.

With this wisdom, I started being more aware during my communications with people and could let go of my judgements and expectations relatively easily. This also allowed me to be completely present with the human being next to me and not be distracted by the endless chatter about the person in my head.

Take Aways

As mentioned before, you are an empty space or no-thing which, in turn, implies that you are timeless and immortal. Thus, what really matters is how you are filling this empty space. Are you allowing the default dialogue that goes inside your head to fill up this space, or are you filling it up with some creative and unique things and endeavours?

Being an empty space also implies that you are beyond any labels. Therefore, the way you see yourself or label yourself plays a crucial role in how you progress in your life. For example, if you say that 'I am too old', 'I am too weak', or 'I am sensitive', then this will become a reality for you because you are who you say you are. The same phenomena will also apply on other people. Meaning, that if you label someone as bossy, demanding, or controlling, then you will always see them as such.

But if you say you are no-thing, then you are like this blank canvas on which anything can be painted. From this space, you can then choose to be anything. You can be strong, timeless, divine, harmonious, etc.

Here is what Nisargadatta Maharaj has to say on the topic of being nothing:

'Wisdom is knowing I am nothing,
Love is knowing I am everything,
and between the two my life moves.'

How to Practise Being Nothing

1. You can start by meditating for shorter time periods. While meditating, listen to the sound of silence. Even if a thought comes up in your mind, don't fight it or run away from it. Just be with it and then gently return back to witnessing the sound of silence.
2. Notice how everything is made up of empty space. Look closely at the objects surrounding you, including your own body. Observe how this empty space fills everything in and around us and still gives us an illusion of everything being solid.
3. Try to remind yourself often that all of us are this empty space or nothingness. While communicating with people in your life, if judgements and expectations show up in your mind, see them as clouds appearing and disappearing in the sky. Remember that these emotions are temporary and you being the limitless sky cannot get affected by them. Choose to let them go and allow your true nature to show up in these circumstances.

Chapter 3

The Act of Allowing

Life is a beautiful journey filled with seemingly different kinds of events which are mystically connected with each other. At any point in our lives, we can either allow life to flow as it intends to or resist its flow. Allowing life to flow as it intends does not mean accepting an unwanted condition in your life out of resignation or because you 'had to' accept it as you ran out of choices. Rather, it's akin to a lotus flower gracefully blossoming amidst murky waters, recognising that the muddy surroundings serve a purpose for its growth.

It's important to realise that allowing life to naturally unfold is essential for our personal growth and expansion. Doing so when life goes our way is quite easy because there is nothing to resist. However, it takes real courage, understanding, and wisdom to allow life to flow when life seems to be not working for us. The twenty-ninth verse of the Tao Te Ching beautifully encapsulates the act of allowing and the perfection of things as they are:

Those who look down upon this world will surely
take hold and try to change things
But this is a plan I've always seen fail
The world is Tao's own vessel
It is perfection manifest
It cannot be changed
It cannot be improved
For those who go on tampering, it's ruined
For those who try to grasp, it's gone
Allow your life to unfold naturally
Know that it too is a vessel of perfection
Just as you breathe in and out
Sometimes you're ahead and other times behind
Sometimes you're strong and other times weak
Sometimes you're with people and other times
alone
To the sage all of life is a movement towards
perfection
So what need has he for the excessive, the
extravagant, or the extreme?

For me personally, allowing life to unfold the way it meant to and not interfering with its natural flow gave me access to unconditional peace and harmony. It allowed me to be completely free by living in the present moment.

The first time the universe showed me what allowing actually implies was when I was moving abroad with my husband. Since this was a huge step for me, I was already under a lot of stress. On top of that, the never-ending stream of questions and advice from every single person around me amplified this pressure. Things like 'Don't forget to pack so and so thing' and 'Make sure to do this and that' really started to take a toll on my mental peace and composure. And no matter how hard I tried to not let it affect me, I still became agitated and angry.

I realised I had to do something about it as I very well knew that this anger was not healthy for me. I tried creating love and acceptance for people around me and myself, but it was to no avail and every time I failed, I blamed myself. This pattern of becoming angry, then trying and failing to find love and acceptance, and consequently blaming myself for it became cyclical.

Unable to sway my emotions in a positive direction or create acceptance, I decided to meditate on the root cause of the problem. I soon realised that it wasn't the fault of people in my life as they were just concerned about me and rather, it was my uncertainty and insecurity about relocating that was reacting to their suggestions and opinions, leading to anger and agitation. And so, in my attempt to make all the correct decisions and not miss out on any important step, I was losing my playfulness and creativity. In short, the more I was trying to get a strong grip on life by controlling the situations and things around me, the more I felt like I was losing control. This may seem paradoxical, but that's how life works.

So, when I stopped worrying and fretting about relocating and everything that comes with it, I experienced a sense of ease and relaxation because now there was nothing to do! In short, I started allowing life to go the way it wanted to go rather than controlling and tampering with it. There was no struggle to have everything in order and no striving for things to happen in a certain way. I was just being and through this, everything was accomplished effortlessly! This is the beauty of allowing life to take its course. And the more you allow it, the more you can see the interconnectedness of all things.

Look around you and notice how the elements in nature thrive just by allowing life to flow through them. Look at a small seed which grows into a vast tree that reaps fruits and flowers. Observe how it never resists life and allows sunshine, rain, and soil to move through it, which helps it to fulfil its true purpose. Imagine, if the seed resisted these forces, could it have ever grown into what it came here to be?

Over the years, we have forgotten this simple act of allowing and have developed a habit of trying to control everything around us. As a result, we often find ourselves struggling. Thus, we have to relearn to trust life and allow it to take its course. Because the more you let go of your desires, the more you allow them to manifest in your life. The opposite is also true. That is, the more we try to hold on to things, the sooner they disappear. In other words, what you resist persists and what you let go manifests! This is the law of the universe.

It is also important to understand that this doesn't mean that we should resign completely and do nothing. There is a subtle difference between 'allowing' and 'resigning'. And you will understand this difference when you start practising the act of allowing. You will experience a lot more fulfilment and ease when you allow things to happen.

Take Aways

Have you ever thought that maybe life is unfolding the way it is meant to, that you are exactly where you are supposed to be and with the people that you are meant to be, and most importantly, that there isn't anything to control or change in life as everything is exactly the way it is supposed to be?

If that's the case, then why do we keep rushing everything? Also, this arduous effort to control life and have things your way only leads to exhaustion and unfulfillment. This is because we face a lot of mental and physical stress due to constantly trying to navigate in the direction we prefer. But once we realise that all things in life flow to their own accord, then we stop wasting our time and energy. Also, once we let go of the need to control everything, then we also attain mental peace and equanimity.

The four noble truths by Buddha mention that it is our clinging and grasping that results in *dukkha* (suffering or discontentment) and that one can end this cycle by just being in the present moment mindfully. And by being in the present moment and allowing life to be can help us live in a liberated state each moment.

> In life, there is suffering, because of the impermanent nature of things.
> Suffering is due to attachments and expectations, to grasping and clinging.
> It's possible to end suffering by giving up attachments (clinging) and expectations (grasping).

How to Practise the Act of Allowing

Given below is a step-by-step guide to help you practice the act of allowing:

1. Observe yourself while you are working to accomplish a certain result. This could be office work or simply some work at your home. Stop for a moment and try experiencing your bodily state. Does your body feel stiff or light?
2. If you feel stiffness and tightness in your body, it is already a sign that you are probably holding on to something, mentally. An important thing to remember here is that if you observe discomfort in your body, it does not mean that there is something wrong with you. It has probably been there for a long time; it is just that you became aware of it now. And now that you are aware, you can do something about it.
3. Bring yourself to the present moment and try loosening your body. Open your hands and mentally imagine letting go of your desired outcome. You can even say this out loud, 'I let go of my attachment to a specific result, and I allow the result to reach me that life intends for me.'

With time and by repeating this practice on a regular basis, you will become more adept at the act of allowing.

Chapter 4

BEING WATER

Lao Tzu mentions at various places in the Tao Te Ching the profound qualities of water and how we can learn from it. Let's take a closer look at the salient features of water mentioned in the book.

- Water truly represents humility—It always seeks the lowest point, demonstrating a natural inclination to yield and adapt.
- It is universal and fundamental—The majority of our body and planet is composed of water and it is one of the most essential sources of energy.
- It is impartial—It nourishes all life without having any preference or bias and treats everyone the same way.
- It is dynamic—It always keeps flowing and there is no obstacle that can hinder its progress.

After reading this, I had the desire to emulate the qualities of water. Soon, I saw an area in my life where I could practise the qualities of water which I had learnt. At the time, I was having a minor conflict with my husband as I felt that he was not contributing enough when it came to doing the household chores. Due to this, I started labelling him as 'unreliable' and 'irresponsible'. But I saw this conflict as an opportunity to put my learnings into practice.

I re-read the eighth verse of the Tao Te Ching over and over again that beautifully captures the wondrous nature of water:

The supreme good is like water,
Which nourishes all things without trying to.
It flows to low places loathed by all men.
Therefore, it is like the Tao.

Live in accordance with the nature of things.
In dwelling, be close to the land.
In meditation, go deep in the heart.
In dealing with others, be gentle and kind.

Stand by your word.
Govern with equity.
Be timely in choosing the right moment.

One who lives in accordance with nature
Does not go against the way of things.
He moves in harmony with the present moment,
Always knowing the truth of just what to do.

This verse really struck me, especially the second stanza, and I started deeply contemplating it in an attempt to actualise it in my life. I began with the first instruction: living in accordance with how things were. So, I slowly started adapting and accepting the fact that even though my request for certain things might not get reciprocated, it was completely fine, and it shouldn't affect me. And just embracing this fact removed a lot of friction and discomfort that I was carrying.

The next step for me was to divide the housework into different slots. I decided to do so after recognising the fact that housework is like any other work, and I had the choice to do a part of it and do the rest later. I also realised that my philosophy of completing everything the same day wasn't conducive and was making me tired. So, I started abiding by the mantra, 'I do not have to do everything today.' This allowed me to prioritise and schedule work while being mindful of my well-being and overall health. This significantly reduced tiredness and fatigue issues which I was having earlier.

I also realised that this idea of 'doing everything right away' was something I was expecting from my husband as well, giving him no freedom or flexibility. After this realisation, I started requesting instead of instructing. This way, he could do the chores in his own way and time. And if he forgot something, then I simply did not complain and did what had to be done. This removed all the resistance from my side and made my husband open up to me about his feelings. He shared with me that initially, he felt a loss of freedom whenever I asked for his help with some housework. But from the time I stopped pressuring him into taking up tasks, he felt more inclined to participate and help me.

This simple act of emulating the qualities of water introduced a sense of freedom for me and my husband. I could recognise the fluidity and flexibility of water flowing in me, and I could share this gift with my husband. Moreover, by being gentle and kind to my own self as well as the people around me, I was able to establish not only a better partnership but also a better relationship with my husband. I am grateful to Lao Tzu for teaching me how I could be water in different areas of my life.

Take Aways

All of us have the capacity to embody the fluidity of water. And if we consider the fact that we are largely made of water, then how difficult can this task be? The fact is that, just like water:

- We too have the ability to be non-judgemental, i.e., treat everyone the same and have no biases.
- We too have the ability to be in a state of flow and overcome all the obstacles in our lives.
- We too have the flexibility to adapt to any situation.

The only thing needed to channel these qualities is to be willing. Once you are willing, you will be shown the way to do it and soon, you will see all your resistance within you dissolve away and you will find an impeccable flexibility within you that will allow you to flow through life without any friction. In a space where there is no resistance, only flow happens!

I truly resonated with the following lines from the novella, *The Penelopiad*, written by Canadian poet, Margaret Atwood, that capture this emotion.

> Water does not resist. Water flows. When you plunge your hand into it, all you feel is a caress. Water is not a solid wall, it will not stop you. But water always goes where it wants to go, and nothing in the end can stand against it. Water is patient. Dripping water wears away a stone. Remember that, my child. Remember you are half water. If you can't go through an obstacle, go around it. Water does.

How to Practise to Be like Water

The first step consists of just interacting with water. Whether you are washing your hands with water or drinking water, just try to be aware of it. The important thing here is that simply by feeling its presence within and outside you will allow you to establish a connection with water. We can also further this connection by expressing our gratitude and thanking it for the gifts it offers to all of us.

The next step involves inquiring about the traits of water you actually want to acquire and how you can introduce them into your life. You can also ask water for its guidance.

After you have learnt the specific traits, work out an area in your life where you can apply these learnings.

1. Before trying to find solutions to any challenge or obstacle, first accept what you have, i.e., the 'what is' of your situation. For example, if a relationship does not work, that means it does not work at this point. It does not mean anything more or anything less and this does not say anything about you or the other person.

   So, it's important to not judge your own situation and instead, try to stay with the situation. Staying with the situation does not mean that you will not take any action to address the issue. Rather, the acceptance of the thing before the addressal is the most important part here. And until and unless you accept what you have, you cannot do something about it.

2. Once you feel you have begun to accept the 'what is' of your situation, question yourself: What is my true commitment in this area?' and 'What am I supposed to do?' And when you do so, keep aside the various conversations happening in your mind like 'Why should I do it?', 'Why can't the other person understand me?' or 'Why did this happen to me?'

3. So, every time there is any kind of disagreement or conflict, try being water. Instead of pushing people to make them understand your point of

view, simply just listen to them without trying to explain or justify your situation or reason. Listening to the other person and letting go of your urge to be heard will create a holistic space for healing the relationship.

Chapter 5

Attachment to Completion

We all seem to be in a rush to complete things as soon as possible and check them off on our to-do lists. And until then, the incomplete tasks haunt us day in and day out. Also, since we all have a never-ending list of things that need to be completed, the thought 'I still have work that needs to be completed' never leaves us. The fact is that this attachment to completion is a very common phenomenon, and it affects many of us. But before we delve into the cause and cure of it, I would like to share how this compulsion personally affected me.

I have always liked researching the topics that I like. And once I have enough material on a particular subject, I would compile a manuscript, covering all my research data. This entire process usually took several years to complete and required me to overcome several challenges. But each time one of my manuscripts was rejected by the reviewers, I would drop everything and go back to it in order to make the necessary amendments and corrections. Even if I had a new proposal to work on, I would leave the work at hand and become totally consumed by the thought of 'completing' the previous manuscript. But why did I feel this need to complete everything? And why did I feel irritated if anything was left incomplete?

After going through this cycle several times, I realised that I was too attached to the closure of things. In other words, I wanted things to just get over or get completed so that I could proceed further. And if anything was left incomplete, it made me feel as if I wasn't progressing further, which, in turn, led to irritation and frustration.

I remember that I would often complain to my husband that I was back to square one and that everything I did earlier was of no use and will have to be done all over again. But was this the truth? Was I really not progressing? Was I really not moving further? And everything that I did earlier was a waste of time and energy?

No . . . it wasn't. And it was the fifteenth verse of the Tao Te Ching that helped me to see this truth.

The ancient masters were profound and subtle.
Their wisdom was unfathomable.
There is no way to describe it.
One can only describe them vaguely by their appearance.

Watchful, like men crossing a winter stream.
Alert, like men aware of danger.
Simple as uncarved wood.
Hollow like caves.

Yielding, like ice about to melt,
Amorphous, like muddy water.

But the muddiest water clears
As it is stilled.
And out of the stillness,
Life arises.

He who keeps the Tao does not want to be full.
But precisely because he is never full,
He can remain like a hidden sprout
And does not rush to early ripening.

These profound words made me realise that it was fine to leave things incomplete. And even though I derived a sense of fulfilment and accomplishment whenever I completed something, doing something only to finish it or accomplish a specific goal takes away the charm and wonder of that task. And this was the exact thing that was happening with me. I would start out with a project because it interested me but soon, my sole purpose would become to complete that particular task. This resulted in me losing the joy and interest that I found in doing something which I loved and instead gave way to stress and frustration.

These lines from Tao Te Ching brought me back to the present moment. I was able to go beyond the surface level and see that every time I thought that I wasn't moving further as there was no result to show for it, in actuality, I was growing and progressing on my path. Each attempt made me learn and grow into a better person and human being. And when I looked back, I could see a cumulative growth in places where I had initially failed.

This learning changed my perspective completely. The line, 'He can remain like a hidden sprout and does not rush to early ripening', really resonated with me and I started applying this ideology in other areas of my life. For example, in the next gardening season, I planted much more flower seeds than the previous season as I was not worried about whether they would bloom or not (which I used to do earlier). I just knew that the growth was happening even though I couldn't see anything on the surface. This realisation put me at ease. And even while gazing at the empty garden that was yet to bloom, I could hear the words, 'Who is to say that there is no growth? Just because I do not see anything on the surface, does not mean that the growth isn't happening. If you move your awareness from the surface and look beneath, all that's happening is growth.'

Take Aways

The most important take away here is that you can never be where you were yesterday as life is evolving every moment. We are changing each moment in our bodies as well as in our minds. Look at the frequency at which your thought changes. Look at how the cells in your body are changing and mutating each moment. Thus, you can never be stagnant or stuck in one place and are always moving ahead on your journey. So, why not live a life in which we do all the things that we are supposed to do but not because we want to finish them or complete them but because we love doing what we do.

How to Practise Detachment from Completion

1. Whenever you feel a compulsion or pressure to complete something, notice how you feel at such times; your bodily state, emotions you experience, all of it. Now ask yourself 'Why do you want to complete these things?' and 'What will happen if you don't complete the task right now?'
2. When something or someone unplanned shows up and disturbs the plan of your day, notice if your urge to complete the tasks you set out to do in the first place clouds your mind and introduces negative emotions. If that's the case, breathe and try cultivating flexibility whenever such a situation arises. See how you can let go of your urge to tick down tasks on your to-do list and adapt to the current situation by re-prioritising.
3. The following practice is something that I recently started doing as a way to diminish my attachment to complete things. I was inspired by the Vietnamese monk, Thich Nhat Hanh, to take this up as a practice. I have a bell alarm on my phone which rings every two hours. And every time it rings, I leave everything and concentrate on my breathing for a few minutes. This way, I come into stillness and silence, putting a halt to the urges to complete the task I had been doing. This conscious stopping also reminds me of the reason why I am doing that

task in the first place and takes me away from the idea of completing it for the sake of it.

Chapter 6

Detachment to Success and Failure

People interpret the word 'detachment' in many different ways. For some, it means ignoring things that they do not like, while for some, it is a state where nothing matters. Well, for me, detachment simply means being present with everything and everyone as they are, without allowing it to affect you.

Tao Te Ching makes several references to the importance of detachment in work as well as in personal life. The second verse of the Tao says:

> The saint inspires the vitality of all lives, without holding back.
>
> He nurtures all beings with no wish to take possession of.
>
> He devotes all his energy but has no intention to hold on to the merit.

> When success is achieved, he seeks no recognition. Because he does not claim for the credit, hence shall not lose it.

The tenth verse also talks about refraining from taking credit once the work is done:

> Giving birth and nourishing; having, yet not possessing; working, yet not taking credit;
>
> leading without controlling or dominating.
>
> One who heeds this power brings the Tao to this very earth. This is the primal virtue.

The concept of detachment has also been mentioned in chapter 18 of the Bhagavad Gita. In this verse, Lord Krishna coaches Arjuna about relinquishing the attachment one has for the results of his actions. He insists that if one simply does their natural duties without any attachment to any outcome, one can go beyond the bondage one experiences in life.

When I first read this verse, my brain said to me, 'This is too difficult for me to practice!' But as always, life gave me an opportunity to implement and live this verse.

This was during the time when I was looking for a job after relocating. Prior to shifting, I had been working for a very long time as I had always liked working and learning new things. But this time, I chose to start my career afresh and so, I was looking for internships in a completely different profession and was preparing for interviews accordingly. But as I was sending my CV to a recruiter, I realised I had no designation to put in my email signature and I felt a bit weird about this fact. I had similar experiences at various meet-up events for building a network. There, I met different people from several industries and these people would introduce themselves as, 'Hey! I am a data scientist and I have eight years of experience,' or 'Hi! I am a software developer and I have been working for ten years.' As for me, in every interaction, I felt like nobody as I had no designation to share with these people.

But the deeper truth was that I had been, unknowingly, seeking validation through a job and without it, I felt as if I was a nobody! So, I started pushing myself even harder to crack an interview and get a job. Also, my strong attachment to this area made me very sensitive to success as well as failure in this area of life. Meaning, that every time I got a call for an interview, I would become immensely happy and on the other hand, whenever I got a rejection, I would become completely dejected. These extreme fluctuations started creating discomfort in me. I could see myself swinging like a pendulum from side to side. I could also see the fact that outside circumstances had the power to shape and influence my life. Basically, a single email or a call from a recruiter had the power to make me sad or happy. This was not what I wanted in my life.

Having this awareness, I stopped and reflected on what was happening. The verses of the Tao showed me that I was associating myself as a function of success and failure. I was letting myself be defined by the title of my job and if the job wasn't there, then it was as if my identity didn't exist anymore due to which I felt lost and unanchored. I also learnt that it was not me who was being successful or failing. In actuality, I was just a divine expression of the universe, and it was the universe that was actually doing things through me.

So, I started practising detachment which involved not taking credit for clearing an interview and not getting affected whenever I failed at an interview. And when I let go of my attachment, I could see that I wasn't the title of my job; I was much more than it. It also allowed me to act on things without the burden or fear of the outcome. Meaning, now I could take all necessary actions to get a job without the need to avoid failures or glorify my past successes to get some kind of validation. And because I had nothing to worry about or lose, I could just focus on taking the necessary actions that were consistent with my commitment. And soon, I started getting calls for several interviews and within a month, I got a job.

Take Aways

You are not defined by the circumstances of your life or anything external in your life. You are life itself. You are the universe. And since the universe is abundant and infinite, then so are you! There is no need for you to chase after anything or attain a specific goal. Your life is perfect in this very moment. Look at nature and see the perfectness of it all. So, if everything around you was made so perfectly, then why do you have to doubt yourself? You too are a perfect being!

One of the beautiful quotations by Sage Vashishtha in the book, *The Himalayan Masters: A Living Tradition*, goes as follows:

If you take your success too seriously, you get entangled and fail to use the objects of your success as a means for the next level of achievement—the spiritual. Thus, right from the beginning of your worldly endeavours, desist from the cravings of the senses and maintain awareness that although the worldly objects provide some degree of comfort, ultimately, they are worthless.

How to Practise Detachment

1. Every time you find yourself chasing something in your life, be it money, relationship, approval from others, etc., just stop and observe yourself. Once you do that, you will see how outside circumstances have total control over our lives. You will also see the absurdity of it all.
2. Then, ask the following question: Who am I? This will make you realise that you are more than your job, identity, relationships, gender . . . more than everything. Even if you do not realise it, keep the question within your heart.
3. Allow everything to reach you without you having to run after it. Remind yourself that everything is moving as per the divine order and whatever is necessary for me will fall back to me eventually.
4. Work for your goals but do not forget your actual motive behind that goal. In other words, work but do not worry about achieving success or avoiding failures.

Chapter 7

Being One with Everything

Human beings normally have a tendency to see things and other people as separate from themselves. This is not surprising as that's what we have been taught. Terms such as he, she, it, they, etc., are used to describe someone outside of us and depict the separation between 'I' and all the other things and beings. But what if there is no separateness? What if there is no I, it, she, he, they, etc.? What if we all are one and connected to each other and this separation is an illusion?

Lao Tzu, in the fifty-fourth verse, explains how Tao is present everywhere:

> The Tao is everywhere;
> It has become everything.
> To truly see it, see it as it is.
> In a person, see it as a person;
> In a family, see it as a family;
> In a country, see it as a country;
> In the world, see it as the world.

How do I know this is true?
By looking inside myself

These lines reveal that everything we see in the physical world emerged from the same empty space . . . the same empty space through which we emerged as well. This means we all are a part of one source!

Let's try to understand this through an example. Once, I was observing a beautiful tree with lush foliage. There were leaves of all shapes and sizes on this tree. And as I was looking at this tree, it led me to the realisation that all the different leaves weren't separate from the tree. Meaning, that the tree was whole and complete and all these seeming separations in the form of leaves were just an illusion. Similarly, all beings in the universe can be considered as the leaves of a tree, and the tree itself as our source.

After this epiphany, I started operating in a different manner in my day-to-day life. My conflicts with people diminished and I started feeling compassion for each and every person that I came across. But this realisation didn't end here. I realised that this oneness does not just include all living things and rather, includes every bit of matter in the universe.

I started putting this realisation into practice and soon, I started seeing cars, traffic lights, my laptop, basically everything as one with me. I recognised the fact that since there is no separation between me and everything else, I can establish a connection with people as well as non-living things and communicate with them. So, when my hair dryer got stuck, I looked at it from a place of oneness and communicated my feelings to it and lo and behold, it started working. Another time, I lost my purse and so I communicated to it that I wanted it to come back to me. Shortly after, it showed up in my life again!

Seeing everything as one dissipated all my fears and gave me a sense of deep comfort. Being in this space enabled me to allow life to flow through me the way it intended to as I knew that life would take care of everyone and everything. I could see the same life that reverberated in me reverberating in other people and things. I could see myself in them and see them in myself! This is one of the most amazing experiences I have had in my life which always brings me into harmony with everything and everyone!

Take Aways

All of us have come from the same source. This source has the capability to yield everything! Also, all the separation we see in life is an illusion and does not exist in reality. The truth is that you are connected to each and everything in this universe. You have the capability to communicate with everything and everyone, no matter how difficult the communication may seem. And sometimes, the communication our inner being establishes with the inner being of the other person is far more powerful than the verbal communication you have. Another important point to note here is that practising this oneness with people does not mean agreeing with or allowing people to step over you. Instead, practising oneness means realising that since we are a part of life, it is always on our side. It also means feeling compassion and connection with everything in life.

Here is what Swami Vivekananda says about oneness:

The Self is the essence of this universe, the essence of all souls; He is the essence of your own life, nay, 'Thou are That.' You are one with this universe. He who says he is different from others, even by a hair's breadth, immediately becomes miserable. Happiness belongs to him who knows this oneness, who knows he is one with this universe.

How to Practise Oneness

1. Look at the things around you and try to see them in a new light. Notice that everything you see, be it a rock, a tree, a table, a pen, or a book, are so different, yet they all have taken birth from the same source. In other words, at the fundamental level, everything is the same.
2. Next, try to establish a connection with any object and communicate with it. An important part of establishing a connection with anything is to be grateful. Acknowledge the stars, the tree, the clouds, the table in your home, the car you drive, etc., for the wonders and value they add to your life.
3. Another thing you can do is speak less and observe more. Normally, each one of us is busy speaking or thinking about the different problems or tasks to be done in our day-to-day lives. This busyness takes away the

opportunity to observe simple things around us. And these simple things hold the secrets of oneness that we fail to see otherwise. Thereby, by not speaking much, you will start to observe more. Also, try to observe other people. Look at them beyond their bodies. Ask yourself who are these people beyond their physical forms and who am I beyond this body? Just asking these questions and being in observance will allow you to see the oneness that surrounds you.

4. Note down your observations and even if there isn't anything worth noting, it's completely fine. Just acknowledge yourself for picking up the exercises in this book. And remember what you have taken up is an extraordinary thing! You are beginning to see beyond what you have been programmed. You are starting to alter your brain patterns. So, it's okay to take time. Do this at your own pace. Just take it slow, one step at a time!

Chapter 8

Communicating with Our Bodies

Our bodies are a magnificent gift from life. They function our entire lives and do all kinds of things without us thinking or knowing about them. Even when asleep, it keeps on working and supervising all the vital functions. So, at times, when I forget who I am and start thinking that 'it is me who has to do everything, otherwise things will not get done', my body reminds me how everything happens inside my body without me trying to accomplish anything! Therefore, if we want to optimise the functioning of our body, i.e., optimise our health, then it is integral to form a bond with our body as it plays an equally important role when it comes to health and well-being. And once this connection is established, we can communicate with our body and the body responds to us with its infinite wisdom.

In the seventy-first verse of the Tao Te Ching, Lao Tzu shares the following lines about what constitutes true health:

> Knowing ignorance is strength.
> Ignoring knowledge is sickness.
> Only when we are sick of our sickness shall
> we cease to be sick.
> The sage is not sick but is sick of sickness;
> this is the secret of health.

The following episode will tell you how these lines completely transformed my life.

> One evening, my husband and I were at a friend's place. During dinner, one of my friends said casually, 'Hey! You seem to put a lot of weight lately.' Now imagine, how that statement could hit a woman. Writing this now, I feel amused by the whole incident but at that moment, I was overcome by self-critical thoughts. I began making harsh and negative evaluations of myself such as 'I have not been taking care of my health', 'I have been eating a lot lately', 'I have failed at finding time to exercise', etc.

Looking back, I can laugh at the absurdity of it all, but like I said, at that moment, it was all real and I struggled to grapple with my emotions. I saw putting on weight as something wrong and felt the need to 'fix' my body.

So, I started doing a lot of high-intensity exercises. But every time I exercised, I felt as if I was pushing too hard. And even if I managed to force myself through the routine, I never felt healthy and at ease. On the other hand, if I missed a day, I would be really critical with myself. Eventually, after a couple of weeks, I decided not to continue with the training. I could sense that something was off inside of me and I was not happy.

This happened a few more times and I found myself in this cycle of criticising my body, then pushing too hard to perform, feeling bad about not achieving the results quickly, and then quitting because it was too much to handle.

After feeling lost and dejected for some time, I remembered the verse mentioned above and the wisdom hidden in it just struck me. I could see the 'sickness' in me and resolved to no longer be sick anymore! That night, I stood in front of a mirror and just looked at my body. I noticed that I had a lot of resistance to look at the fat of my body, to see my body out of proportion. But I kept looking at it. I touched my body, especially my stomach (because I was trying too hard to push my stomach back in to look slim and beautiful) and then said sorry to my body. At that moment, I had tears in my eyes, and I saw what I had been doing with my body.

Our bodies have a wonderful feature: they communicate to us when we are out of alignment with our own selves. For instance, our bodies becoming fat is a signal to let us know that we have not been mindful in our lives. This can include not being mindful enough to see what we are ingesting, not being mindful enough of the kind of thoughts we are entertaining, etc.

My body was telling me the same. It was communicating that it needed support. And instead of listening to it, what I did was put more pressure on it, hoping that this would make it function at an optimal level. I also realised that I had so much dislike for the current state of my body because of which I wanted to get into a better shape as quickly as possible which, in turn, was the reason why I just kept pushing my body and doing everything possible to lose weight.

It's worth noting that I am not suggesting that we should do nothing if our bodies are becoming unfit. Rather, what I am trying to convey is that the bodies we have are a wondrous gift and it is absolutely important to take care of them. And exercising is one such tool that can help us maintain our health and keep our body functioning properly. I too was taking all necessary action to get in shape, but behind these actions, there was a lot of dislike for the way my body looked or had become. There was resistance and an urge to fix it immediately as if it was not already doing enough for me. I also did not have enough compassion for my body to listen to what it was trying to communicate.

All these realisations really opened my eyes and made me see my health and my body in a completely new light. So, that day, standing in front of the mirror, I said to my body, 'I am sorry that I did not listen to you, but I am here for you now. Please tell me, how can I help you?' This time, it was not about losing that extra weight to look beautiful, but it was more about how can I take care of this beautiful gift that I have been bestowed with by the universe.

At that moment, I remember that I sensed a lot of ease in me. And though nothing had changed as such—I still had a lot of extra weight on my body—I felt peaceful because the resistance or the urge to fix my body vanished. The only thing that remained was immense gratitude for my body and a desire to support it to get back to its natural state.

The next day, miraculously, I came across a video—even though I had not been searching for it—in which Dr Wayne Dyer spoke about how he could maintain his health by cutting down on sugar. After I saw the video, I immediately knew that it was my body's way to let me know how I could take care of it.

So, I started monitoring my sugar intake and became more mindful of what I was eating. Every time I picked something at the grocery store, I would check its contents to see how much sugar it contained. I also became more conscious of providing my body with all nutrients. I was also mindful of not limiting myself to a prison of 'I should not eat sugar at all'. So, I would have ice creams sometimes and not get too stressed out or bound by my own rules. Along with this dietary regime, I also regularly exercised and did not unnecessarily push myself too hard.

An important thing to note here is that introducing a new regime can be initially difficult for our body to adapt to because of its prior conditioning and the habits that we have followed for a long time. Therefore, it is necessary to bring about this change not drastically but one step at a time. This is another way of showing compassion to your body. Ultimately, this regime worked for me as I lost the extra weight and now, I feel a lot healthier and more active.

Take Aways

If there is one thing that I would like you to take away from this chapter is that being healthy is not about having six-packs or a slim figure. Rather, it is about how mindful we are in our day-to-day life about our requirements and what it is trying to communicate. And for this, we need to form a bond with our bodies.

The first step to initiate communication with our bodies is to first acknowledge that we have one! Understand and appreciate the nature of our bodies and see how complex, intricate, and wonderous they are. And once we start doing so, our bodies will respond, and we will begin to understand what it is saying. Clarissa Pinkola Estés, the author of the bestselling book, *Women Who Run with the Wolves: Myths and Stories of the Wild Woman Archetype*, beautifully encapsulates this sentiment.

> The body is a multilingual being. It speaks through its colour and its temperature, the flush of recognition, the glow of love, the ash of pain, the heat of arousal, the coldness of non-conviction. It speaks through its constant tiny dance, sometimes swaying, sometimes a—jitter, sometimes trembling. It speaks through the leaping of the heart, the falling of the spirit, the pit at the centre, and rising hope. The body remembers, the bones remember, the joints remember, even the little finger remembers. Memory is lodged in pictures and feelings in the cells themselves. Like a sponge filled with water, anywhere the flesh is pressed, wrung, even touched lightly, a memory may flow out in a stream.

How to Communicate with Your Body

1. Take out some time to acknowledge and feel the presence of your body. Close your eyes and feel your hands. See how much assistance your hands provide in your daily life. Now do the same for every part of your body—your heart, stomach, intestines, lungs, etc. The main objective of this activity is to feel and acknowledge the various parts of your body and generate gratitude for them for the work they do for us.
2. Show compassion and gratitude to your body by thinking or saying positive affirmations such as, "Thank you for what you have been doing for me and I am grateful to you.' You can take this communication further by asking questions like, 'How can I help you?', 'How can I support you?', and 'How can I make you healthy?' Remain aware of your true self and the nature of your physical body, and you will be provided with answers.
3. Next, you can focus on the aspects of your body that you want to improve. For example, if you have pain in your back, close your eyes and try to experience your back and listen to what it is trying to say. Show your appreciation in the form of positive thoughts for the role it plays in your life.

Chapter 9

Going beyond Uncertainty

Life can be quite uncertain. The fact is that nobody knows what is going to happen the next moment. And due to this uncertainty, we all constantly experience fear about what might happen. In other words, we experience a fear of 'what ifs'. But on the flip side, we will find that it is this uncertainty that makes our lives adventurous and full of excitement.

Imagine, if we knew everything about our futures, everything that is going to happen in the next moment, how boring our lives would be!

Lao Tzu, in the first verse of the Tao Te Ching, talks about how being with the 'mystery', i.e., situations where we 'do not know' or 'cannot see clearly', can actually enable us to resolve all life's mysteries.

> The Tao that can be told,
> Is not the eternal Tao
> The name that can be named
> Is not the eternal name.

The Tao is both named and nameless
As nameless it is the origin of all things
As named, it is the mother of 10,000 things.

Ever desireless, one can see the mystery;
Ever desiring, one sees only the manifestations
And the mystery itself is the doorway to all
understanding.

As for me, I always felt a loss of strength and confidence within me when it came to dealing with uncertainty. And every time I found myself in a situation where I didn't know what had to be done next, a debilitating fear would crop up and take hold of me. But I also knew that fear is an emotion that is a natural part of human beings and there is no way to get rid of it completely. Also, the more we try to remove something, the more it grows. So, I decided to work on accepting and becoming comfortable with this fear of uncertainty.

I took up the habit of getting up early in the morning, around 5:30 a.m., and going for a bike ride in the nearby forest. During these early hours, the sun wasn't up and there would be pitch-black darkness, especially in the forest. Apart from the harnessing will to get up early morning and step out in the chilly weather, the biggest resistance I felt to achieve my objective was from the darkness outside. And though I had a bike light with me so that I could bike safely and mindfully in the forest, it didn't help with the fear of the unknown and uncertainty that I felt by being alone in the forest. Kindly note that I took this decision of going out in the dark as the area where I lived and biked was very safe and I strongly advise everyone to be mindful of their safety if they wish to do the same. Having said that, let's get back to the story.

After biking for some time, I started noticing certain patterns within me. I noticed that when I biked on some trails where there was light, I would become more relaxed. But when it came to trails with no light, I would bike very quickly to get past the dark trail as soon as possible.

I wanted to know the cause of this behaviour and so, I asked myself: Why do I repel darkness and what makes me afraid of it? After some contemplation, I realised that the fear of darkness stems from the fact that darkness represents uncertainty. Basically, just as we cannot see what lies ahead in the dark, we also do not know what's going to happen in the coming moment and this gives rise to the aforementioned fear. But does it mean that we always have to fear and repel darkness?

One day, while biking in the forest, I entered a dense patch where I could see only a small portion of the trail with my bike light. And as I peddled through this trail, I realised that the thing I was most afraid of was not being able to see everything ahead of me. And bam! At that moment, the entire thing clicked, and I realised that this is exactly what happens in our lives. We get overwhelmed or anxious when we do not see or know what lies ahead of us in life. And it is this fear of not knowing that scares us as it makes us feel that we are not in control.

The next day, when I went out, I experienced something that I cannot express in words completely. Being mindful of what I discovered, as soon as I came on the trail where there was no light, instead of biking too fast, I slowed down and started relaxing my body. As a result, I felt absolutely safe. I could sense the universal power being there with me as a guardian. And if the source, which has created everything, was there to take care of me, then how could I be afraid of what I could see and what I could not?

This insight filled me with trust, gratitude, and love for the universe and I noticed that I was no longer afraid of darkness. It was not that now I was not being mindful of going into the dark but somehow, the resistance to it dissolved at that moment for me.

This beautiful experience helps me today as well when dealing with situations in my life where I do not know everything. Knowing that I am being supported by this higher power turns me into a more relaxed being.

Take Aways

'Knowing' and 'not knowing' are simply two states of our mind. But these states are temporary and you will find yourself oscillating between them. For example, we all have been in situations where we know what to expect next and how to deal with what's coming up. But then there are times when we find ourselves completely clueless and without any certainty about the best way forward.

Thus, instead of always striving and struggling to know and reach somewhere, we should learn to accept the fact that we will never know it all. All we need to do is have faith in the universe and know that it has our back. This will help us overcome the fear of uncertainty by grounding us in life and making us more relaxed and content.

A quotation by Rainer Maria Rilke, an 18th-century poet, from the book, *Letters to a Young Poet,* (translated by M. D. Herten Norton) beautifully captures this sentiment.

> Be patient toward all that is unsolved in your heart and try to love the questions themselves like locked rooms and like books that are written in a very foreign tongue. Do not now seek the answers, which cannot be given you because you would not be able to live them. And the point is, to live everything. Live the questions now. Perhaps you will then gradually, without noticing it, live along some distant day into the answer.

How to Be Okay with Not Knowing

1. Write down in your journal all the areas or aspects of your life where you have a fear of not knowing and uncertainty. This can include things like your work, marriage, relationships, kids, finances, etc.
2. You can use the sentence structure as 'I do not know how to . . .' or 'I have no idea when to . . .' You can create your custom sentences here.
3. Read this list 5-10 times out loud until you become okay with the uncertainty embedded in these statements. You will notice that this is

what actually is! This is what you have in the present moment and no amount of discomfort, frustration, or complaint can change it. Simply put, there are things that you know and then there are things which you don't know.

4. Now, given what you know or what you can see in this area, just take the first step exactly how you would have while driving on an unknown road. Don't take too much time analysing each and every part of your journey or planning the future. Simply by taking small steps, we will gradually reach a place of clarity.

Chapter 10

Running behind the Unreal

Some of the most pertinent questions of life are 'What is real and what is unreal?' and 'How can we know real from unreal?' I consider only our authentic self as being real. Our inner being has an amazing way of letting us know what is real and what is unreal. You and I always know it. But the question is are we willing to listen to the truth our inner being is telling us? Or are we still running behind the unreal? If you find yourself in this situation, you might frequently feel fatigued, burdened with numerous responsibilities, and compelled to achieve external outcomes. In such a state, a sense of unfulfillment may persist, and there will always be a need to find some place or goal which is distant from you, where you need to reach because only then you can feel fulfilled.

In the forty-fourth verse of the Tao Te Ching, Lao Tzu asks us:

> Which means more to you,
> You or your renown?

Which brings more to you,
You or what you own?
I say what you gain
Is more trouble than what you lose.

Reflecting on this verse, I came to the realisation that there's a distinction between myself and the possessions I have. I realised that it's within my control to choose where I direct my attention: towards the ephemeral and ever-changing external world or towards my eternal, unchanging inner self. This choice ultimately shapes the path of my life and influences the degree of fulfilment and tranquillity I experience in it.

A few days ago, I found myself experiencing discomfort while working with a colleague. Despite taking some initial steps to address the issue, the discomfort would often resurface over time. I couldn't understand why I seemed to stumble and feel confused when interacting with this colleague. It would have been easy to place the blame on my colleague's behaviour, assuming that they were the cause of my discomfort. However, this approach did not align with my commitment to maintaining a productive and harmonious working relationship, as it would have led to an endless cycle of blame and guilt, ultimately affecting our team's work.

So, I decided to delve deeper into the situation. When I stopped searching for answers externally, I began to find them within myself. That night, I felt unsettled because I couldn't pinpoint the source of my discomfort at work. I decided to meditate before going to sleep. As I have mentioned before, the universe often communicates with us through our dreams, reflecting our current life experiences. That night, in my dream, I saw myself frantically collecting beautiful, sparkling earrings, trying to keep them safe to prevent any loss. These earrings weren't even real; they were just artificial pieces I had purchased. Despite this, I couldn't help but try to protect them. In my eagerness to gather them, I placed them in a bag, only to have the bag tear, causing me to lose the earrings. Then, I heard a voice behind me saying, 'Why are you working so hard? You can find all these earrings in the next shop.' It was at that moment I woke up from my dream with a big smile on my face. I understood the message the universe had conveyed.

Just as in the dream, I had been preoccupied with safeguarding something unreal—my 'image'—when working with my colleague. I had become too attached, fearing that my colleague was constantly judging me. However, I came to realise that I am not my image. Regardless of what happens to this image, I remain unaffected because nothing can harm my true self. Once again, I saw myself as an empty space where events unfolded, but these events had no bearing on my 'self'. My true self, as an empty space, remained untouched and unaffected by the occurrences within that space.

The following day, I had a candid conversation with my colleague and shared my experiences at work. Instead of placing blame, I took responsibility for my discomfort and asked my colleague how we could work together to find a solution that would allow me to contribute fully to the team. When I started to be authentic and vulnerable, we were able to communicate with compassion and understanding. In this space, I felt no fear because my focus had shifted to my timeless being, and I was no longer identifying my 'self' with my 'image'. I had nothing to cling to or protect. I could simply be. As a result, my colleague began making efforts to foster a culture of collaboration where I could reach out freely and work effectively.

Take Aways

It is important for one to distinguish between what is real and what is unreal. If we keep running behind the unreal things in our lives, we can end up feeling unfulfilled, empty, and purposeless. This might seem like no matter how much you strive, your thirst for satisfaction is never quenched. And whenever you find yourself in such a spot, it is important to remind yourself that your true essence is akin to an empty space, impervious to harm. Regardless of how fast you run or how tightly you cling to things or people you fear losing, life unfolds as it is meant to. Each event in your life is not merely a coincidence but a purposeful path leading you to where you are destined to be.

Remember that you always have a choice. You can either fixate on or cherish the unreal aspects of your life, or you can recognise and embrace your authentic self, living in alignment with it.

Chasing after the unreal or desperately holding onto something you desire intensely will only result in more running, fatigue, and discomfort. In this very moment, you possess the power to either be confined or to experience the boundless and infinite nature of your true self. The fact is that true fulfillment, ease, and contentment only manifest when we can distinguish between these two realms. And when you let go, you will notice that life will either align precisely with your desires or you will begin to desire life's natural course. In either scenario, you will experience profound fulfilment and inner peace.

Nisargadatta Maharaj in his book, *I Am That* wrote edifying lines describing what is real and what is unreal:

> The real does not die, the unreal never lived.
>
> Once you know that death happens to the body and not to you, you just watch your body falling off like a discarded garment.
>
> The real you is timeless and beyond birth and death. The body will survive as long as it is needed. It is not important that it should live long.

How to Distinguish the Real from the Unreal

1. Take a moment to examine your surroundings and contemplate the nature of everything you see. Dive deep into the essence of the objects around you, the events that have unfolded in your life, the individuals who have crossed your path, and even consider the nature of your own physical body. Observe the constant state of change inherent in all these elements. Recognise that something so transient cannot be deemed as real. Reflect upon a fundamental question: Amidst all this perpetual change, is there something that remains constant in your

life? Something that has been a consistent presence since you first became aware of yourself. Acknowledge that it is you who has always been with yourself throughout this journey. Even during moments when you felt utterly alone, you were still in your own company. Embark on an inquiry to understand the essence of this 'you'. Is it your body, your mind? If not, then who is this you?

2. Next, pay close attention to yourself whenever you encounter discomfort. Examine whether you feel fatigued or notice any signs of clinging or grasping in your behaviour. Ask yourself what it is that you are holding onto so tightly. What is causing the fear of loss? Remind yourself that you are a timeless being. Nothing can truly depart from you or enter into you, as everything already exists within you. Your identity is not rooted in these external things or events but resides in the space within which all of this unfolds. In conclusion, be mindful to focus on the timeless being rather than the things/events which are bound by time.

Chapter 11

The Art of Non-interference

For the majority of people, the definition of non-interference would be along the lines of either being indifferent or just minding one's own business. And earlier, I too had the same preconceived notions about what non-interference meant. However, this concept took a whole new meaning when I was reading Tao.

The forty-eighth verse of the Tao Te Ching beautifully captures the idea of non-interference:

> Learning consists of daily accumulating.
>
> The practice of the Tao consists of daily diminishing; decreasing and decreasing, until doing nothing.
>
> When nothing is done, nothing is left undone.
>
> True mastery can be gained by letting things go their own way. It cannot be gained by interfering.

Also, in the thirty-second verse, Lao Tzu further elaborates on the importance of practising the virtue of non-interference:

> The universal Tao has no name.
>
> Although It appears in the plainest and may seem small, It is inferior to nothing.
>
> If the kings and marquises can abide by the Great Tao, All beings shall act as guests and submit to them.
>
> Heaven and earth will then be in harmony and shall descend sweet dew.
>
> People will not require command and orders, yet can treat each other equally with peace.
>
> When Tao is manifested, names were given for the purpose of distinction.
>
> But one must know how to attain the original pureness in order to avoid danger and disaster. Tao exists in the universe like the rivers and streams that lead to the ocean.

When I first read Tao Te Ching, I could not completely comprehend the concept of non-interference as laid out in the book. For example, as per the book, if our governments practise non-interference, it will result in a whole new harmonious world. This was very counterintuitive for me as I thought that in order for things to be harmonious, the government's active participation and interference were absolutely required.

The root cause of this conception was that for me, non-interference meant resignation from life and it had a negative connotation. It is because we are always told that we should actively participate in every facet of life, and we should take every matter into our own hands. In such an environment, the idea of not interfering with life and letting things find their own course can be seen as a surrendering and indolent attitude. And this was the exact perception I held about this concept for the longest time. But this was about to change.

I had taken up gardening as part of a meditation exercise. And even though I had no prior experience, I decided to plant a tulip flower in order to experience the flow of life. I was excited to do something new, but I noticed that I was a bit worried as well.

Soon after, I noticed that birds were coming over and tampering with the plant. As a result, I became an overprotective guardian of the plant. I would constantly check it and make the necessary adjustments and improvements, thinking I was taking care of the plant.

It then became clear to me that I had developed an attachment to the tulip. Realising this, I started practising non-interference. After practising non-interference for some time, I discovered a new meaning of the term and saw it in a completely new light. Now, for me, non-interference means doing what I am supposed to do but not because of any kind of attachment or because I want someone or something to be a certain way! It means that I can give the other person complete freedom to be who they are and yet continue doing my part. And this is what Lao Tzu meant when he spoke about non-interference.

As per him, non-interference is when people are not forced to do things or told what they need to do, but still everyone knows and does exactly what they are supposed to do.

I returned to gardening with this new-found understanding. My commitment to take care of the plant was still there, however, I gave the plant the choice to live or die. This decision allowed me to take care of the plant and perform all the necessary care tasks but released me from the attachment to the expectation that the plant must blossom and thrive in a certain way. And when I gave up my attachment to the plant being the way I wanted it to be, it started flourishing. A green leafy stem soon sprouted, and the plant started to grow and bloom.

I still have this tulip plant and I give my love to it every time I see it.

Take Aways

Non-interference means giving the freedom to life to flow the way it wants to. When I say life, it includes everything and everyone in it. In this space, there are no 'should' or 'should not'. In other words, there are no boundations that you put on life. When life is free to move in the manner it wants to, it then flows in a way that results in your highest good. Also, non-interfering does not mean giving up your own nature or who you are. Rather, it is about being flexible and unattached so that you can be who you are meant to be and do what you are supposed to do. In other words, non-interference means accepting anything and everything with open arms because everything comes from the universe.

Having said that, I would like to remind you all that acceptance of everything does not mean agreeing or tolerating someone's unpleasant behaviour; rather, it is the acceptance of the nature of the situation and then doing what you are supposed to do.

In his book, *I Am That*, Nisargadatta Maharaj shares the following dialogue:

> Refuse all thoughts except one: the thought 'I am'. The mind will rebel in the beginning, but with patience and perseverance it will yield and keep quiet. Once you are quiet, things will begin to happen spontaneously and quite naturally without any interference on your part.

How to Practise Non-interference

1. Non-interference can be practised in various scenarios of life. For example, whenever you have a conflict, look into what the conflict is about. What do you want from this conflict? Do you want to win the argument, or do you want harmony? If it's the former option, then that means you want to have control and have things and people be in a certain way. But if you want harmony, you will have to learn to allow people to be the way they want to be. Trust them as they too have infinite wisdom and are continuously being guided by life. When you let go of control, you will create a space where harmony will start to fill in.

2. Another situation where you can practise non-interference is when someone close to you reaches out to you for advice. When such a situation presents itself, observe the moment and withdraw from giving any advice. Say to the other person, 'I trust you and I know you are abundantly wise.' Ask them questions rather than suggesting solutions; questions that will have them create a solution of their own. This will allow the people in your life to develop trust in themselves. Practising non-interference in such a situation will also diminish your ego that wants to experience glory by suggesting and advising people!

Chapter 12

Transcending Morality and Ethics

Principles of morality, ethics, and virtue are much debated, and rightly so, because they entail a deeper dimension than just what is right or what is wrong. So, let's peel the layers and take a closer look to better understand the true nature of these principles.

Lao Tzu explains these principles in a lucid manner in the eighteenth verse of the Tao Te Ching:

> When the greatness of the Tao is present,
> Action arises from one's own heart.
> When the greatness of the Tao is absent,
> Actions comes from the rules
> of kindness and justice.
>
> If you need rules to be kind and just,
> If you act virtuously
> This is a sure sign that virtue is absent.

Thus, we see the great hypocrisy.

When kinship falls into discord,
Piety and rites of devotion arise.
When the country falls into chaos,
Official loyalists will appear.
Patriotism is born.

This is one of the most profound verses of the Tao. And though, at first glance, some parts of it might seem contradictory, the fact is that, on the whole, it provides a very insightful perspective on the principles of morality and virtue. It says that when people are not living from the Tao, rules will be required to specify and state how to be kind, just, and noble. And once rules are needed to ordain morality and ethics, then it can only be false morality and ethics, as true morality and righteousness can only arise in the heart and not be enforced. Now let's unpack this idea in simpler terms.

In short, morality pertains to operating in an ideal way in society. And while this moral framework is very useful in building a functional society, the issues crop up when we 'try' to be moral instead of 'being' moral. This is because trying often implies there is a distorted reason behind the intention to be moral. So, we can see that morality can never be forced and has to come organically. All this might seem a bit confusing and abstract at first, but I would request you to read this over and over again to see the underlying message here and reflect on how this verse shows up in your life. Let me share how this verse completely transformed my professional and personal life.

Morality often comes bundled with a list of 'shoulds' and 'should nots' that dictate a standard we are expected to adhere to. As humans, we frequently conform to these societal rules to meet the expectations set before us. However, in this pursuit, we often lose sight of the true essence of morality. With this verse in mind, I began to notice a certain behaviour in myself at work.

Initially in my career, I would tightly cling to these 'shoulds' and 'should nots'. I was juggling multiple projects, each with its own set of deadlines, and I observed that the pressure associated with these timelines was causing me significant discomfort. And in order to be seen as a helpful team member, I rushed to complete each task as swiftly as possible and eagerly sought out additional work. While there is nothing inherently wrong with being efficient or assisting one's team, I couldn't ignore the underlying pressure and unease I felt.

Despite my initial rationalisations that I was being a kind and supportive team player, deep down, something didn't sit right. After careful reflection, I realised I was striving to meet a series of predefined standards, guided by a set of 'shoulds' and 'should nots', in order to align with the image of a good employee. According to these beliefs, a good employee should be efficient at completing tasks, handle deadline pressure effortlessly, and always be ready to help their colleagues when they need support.

My discomfort stemmed from this relentless pursuit of these standards, and it became evident that my true intent to help the team had been overshadowed.

Once again, it had become more about me than about genuinely assisting others. In this new light, I began to pose different questions to myself. I asked, 'Why am I working with this team?', 'Who am I truly contributing to?', and 'How can I truly assist people in my team?' Considering these questions completely changed my perspective, and my experience transformed entirely.

I continued to work on the same projects, but now there was no pressure to complete the project for the sake of it. The focus shifted to the tasks themselves, which, as it turned out, were not as daunting as they had seemed under the weight of expectations. This way I became more efficient and effective at completing my tasks.

I remained supportive of my team, but now it was a mindful act. I evaluated my bandwidth before taking on additional tasks, and if necessary, communicated my limitations to the team. I also recognised the importance of taking breaks to prioritise my well-being.

Simply put, my motivation shifted from working because I felt obligated to adhere to certain rules because I was genuinely committed to serving my fellow human beings. This newfound perspective not only empowered me in my professional life but also significantly impacted my personal relationships, where I had often grappled with the pressure of being the perfect wife, daughter, or daughter-in-law.

Take Aways

Striving for moral and ethical behaviour is not bad, but it becomes limiting if you simply carry out certain actions because you want to be moral and do not recognise the actual context behind those actions. Simply put, when you live from a place of good or bad, right or wrong, etc., you confine yourself in a limited world and miss out on the bigger picture. Also, this kind of perception of morality and ethics leads to a binary segregation, i.e., one person is good, and the other person is bad. In such a space, where there is duality or separation, only false or insincere morality can exist.

However, when you go beyond these ideas of right and wrong, you will find a more authentic way of living and more opportunities and possibilities will emerge in this space!

In his book, *Yoga Morality: Ancient Teachings at a Time of Global Crisis*, Georg Feuerstein echoes a similar idea about what true morality entails in the yogic world:

> In its goal of radical self-transcendence, Yoga even intends to reach beyond the level of normative behaviour or learned morality. In order to live authentically, the sages insist, we must transcend the human-made categories of 'good' and 'evil', which vary from culture to culture, even sometimes from group to group.

How to Go Beyond Morality and Ethics

1. Write down the standards and rules that you have defined for yourself. In short, the shoulds and the should nots through which you live your life. Notice where you feel limited by these standards which you are continuously trying to meet.

2. To liberate yourself from these constraints, ask yourself: 'Why am I adhering to these standards and not introducing flexibility?', 'What do I want to truly achieve/fulfil?', and 'What is my hidden agenda here—is it about me or them?'.
3. Continue going deeper with these questions. For example, if you have no hidden agenda, then what's your primary goal in this area and what is required to achieve that? You can take this further by asking yourself how can you do this task harmoniously while not pressurising yourself and also taking care of the people involved in this situation.

If you feel a lot of conflicts in your mind or feel overwhelmed by these questions, work on first relaxing your body and mind before going into self-enquiry. Self-enquiry can be done relatively easily when the mind and body are relaxed. There are a number of ways through which you can relax your body and mind. For example, take deep breaths consciously, go for a hike in nature, participate in an outdoor sport, or take up yoga or any activity that relaxes. Most importantly, remember we do not have to get all the answers in one day. Just keep working on them one by one and soon you will find clarity on the best way to achieve your goals and live your life to the fullest.

Chapter 13

Loving the Enemy

The phrase 'Loving the enemy' might stir various reactions in different individuals. Some might dismiss it as an impractical or absurd concept, while others could choose to overlook it entirely. I, too, once regarded it as an unattainable notion until I embarked on a journey of contemplation and examined its presence in my own life. But before I share my story, let's explore this from the start.

Who is an enemy to you? Is it someone who you feel threatened by or someone you feel may hurt you? Maybe the word enemy is a bit too strong, but I am talking about those people in your life for whom you don't have much love. With some of them, you might have minor friction but with some, there might be a lot of animosity. In all these cases, the common thread is that there is a lack of love. But what does 'love' mean to you? Does it mean being nice at all times? Or does it mean having an agreement or common ground with someone? Is love conditional or is it unconditional?

Lao Tzu, in the fifth verse of the Tao Te Ching, magnificently describes the essence of unconditional love.

Heaven and earth are impartial;
they see the 10,000 things as straw dogs.
The sage is not sentimental; he treats all his people as straw dogs.
The sage is like heaven and earth:
To him none are especially dear, nor is there anyone he disfavours.
He gives and gives, without condition, offering his treasures to everyone.
Between heaven and earth is a space like a bellows;
empty and inexhaustible, the more it is used, the more it produces
Hold on to the centre. Man was made to sit quietly and find the truth within.

The first few lines of the verse really struck a chord with me. It completely changed the way I looked at the world around me and my ideas of how to love. Let's explore this further.

In this verse, what Lao Tzu is asking us to do is be impartial, i.e., treat everyone—in fact, everything and every situation—the same way. But is this really possible? Can we treat our loved ones and the people we don't resonate with the same way? I understand that for many, answering this question with a clear yes or no would be difficult. But what I did get from this verse was that it is indeed possible to find love within ourselves for all people and things in life. It all depends on how you define love. For me, love involves understanding the way someone or something is and having compassion for them the way they are. And the more we practise this, the better we get at harnessing and sharing this unconditional love.

However, practising such unconditional love became particularly difficult during the coronavirus pandemic. It was the beginning of March 2020, and I was feeling all the symptoms of the virus. But I could not go to the doctor because of the shortage of test kits in the country and due to strict regulations that were imposed at the time. The inability to consult a doctor was upsetting for me. This situation was further exacerbated by the panic and uncertainty circulating among people. Everywhere I went and everyone I spoke to only brought more negative and pessimistic energy into my life. Soon, I found myself becoming a part of bleak and cynical conversations such as how the virus was wreaking havoc in the lives of people the world over and how it was the cause of innumerable catastrophes.

This continued for some time and during this time, I found myself depleted, tired, and exhausted very often. Amusingly, I was blaming everything on the virus. But then I came upon the realisation that I needed to stop and listen to what was happening inside of me. I closed my eyes and sensed a lot of fear and anger inside of me as I believed that the virus was responsible for disrupting all our lives and the whole economy. And at that moment, Lao Tzu's words echoed in my mind, resonating like the clear chime of a bell!

> The sage is not sentimental; he treats all his people as straw dogs.

He gives and gives without condition, offering his treasures to everyone.

I then asked myself, 'I have been practising to include everyone and everything in the purview of my unconditional love so then why was I excluding the virus?' I could see that the only relationship I had with the virus was that of fear and hatred and I was resisting it with my full strength. And then it dawned on me why I had been feeling tired and exhausted. This constant push back and resistance were taking up all my strength and hence, causing tiredness in my body.

That day, I sat down and tried to create a new relationship with the virus. I noticed that the entire human race was directing its anger and fear against this entity and considered it an enemy. An important point to note here is that I wasn't trying to be in favour of or against the virus. My intention was to see it for what it was and deal with it accordingly. So, I closed my eyes and felt the virus in and around me. I saw it as a living being (which it actually is!) trying to do what it is supposed to and there is nothing wrong with that. It wasn't that it intentionally wanted to disrupt the world and cause harm to humanity.

So, while sitting there, I asked myself if I could be non-sentimental and see the virus in a neutral light and whether I could stop directing fear and anger towards this entity and give out something else. And then suddenly, I saw the virus as a living organism. And as I gained insight into the situation's purpose, I began to extend love and understanding to its inherent nature, realising that my anger or fear held no power to resolve anything.

Kindly note that this didn't mean that I stopped taking all the necessary precautions to keep myself and my surroundings safe. The only thing that changed was that all my actions now originated from a place of non-judgement rather than fear or anger. I could just see the virus as what it was and stopped blaming it as a cause of dysfunction in my life.

Now, I no longer feared the virus or harboured anger towards it. I embraced responsibility and fulfilled my duty as a human being to contribute to the planet's safety. By 'holding onto my centre', as Lao Tzu suggests, I discovered a profound truth within myself: we all have the capacity to extend unconditional love to everyone, including those we perceive as enemies!

Take Aways

The most important take away here is to understand the true definition of love. Love does not necessarily mean that we have to be in agreement with someone even when we don't feel like it. And when we step out into this world, we are sure to find many people who don't elicit the love that we have for our friends and family. But in such cases, even if we manage to sow a small seed of love for the other person, then we can see and understand why the other person is the way they are. And once this happens, we generate compassion for them, or in other words, dissolve our hatred or anger.

Louise Hay, a world-renowned author, talks about what unconditional love looks like in her book, *Dissolving Barriers*:

If I want to be loved as I am,
I have to be willing to love others as they are.

How to Cultivate Love for Everyone

The following exercise will help you to overcome resistance you might have towards accepting and loving someone.

1. Find a quiet space. Sit there and make yourself comfortable.
2. Close your eyes and breathe a couple of breaths mindfully.
3. Now visualise the person that really hurt you or that person whom you consider to be your enemy. Look into their eyes and try to relate to them. See the humanity in them; a person who loves, gets angry, gets sad, has aspirations and dreams, etc.
4. Next, visualise that you are either holding their hand or hugging them, whatever feels comfortable to you.
5. Then say, 'I am willing to understand you. I know I felt hurt by you, but I am willing to let this hurt go. Thank you for coming into my life to teach this lesson to me. I now let you go.'
6. Repeat this exercise a few times and I am sure that it will bring a lot of love and ease into your life.

Chapter 14

Nurturing Humility

Humility is one of the most cited virtues in many ancient texts. The Tao Te Ching also exposits the nature of humility and what it means to be humble. The twenty-eighth verse of the Tao reads as follows:

> To know the strong masculine principle yet abide by the gentle female principle is like being the valley of the world where all rivers will flow into.
>
> This is alike all virtue which will merge into the subtle Tao.
> Being a valley of the world and not depart from the true nature, one can return to original pureness like an infant.
> When one knows the white that is splendour, yet holds on to the black that is humble and lowly. He can be a standard of the world. Being a standard of the world and not deviate from true nature, one is able to return to the void of Tao.

To know what is honour, yet abide by the dishonoured, is like a valley of the world which is modest and humble.

Being the valley of the world makes possible the true virtue to be complete and sufficient.

And hence can return to simplicity.

When the nature of simplicity is being manifested, it results into various vessels.

And by applying the pure simplicity, a saint can master all things.

Hence, the Great Tao is a unified Oneness which cannot be separated apart.

I never actually understood the real meaning of humility until I read this verse. As a child, I was a talkative and extroverted person. I really liked getting attention from people around me and thus, I would always take an active approach to achieve the same. I also thought that being solitary, timid, and lowly was a sign of having low confidence.

So, when I started practising this verse, I felt a certain resistance in me because I thought that in order to imbibe the virtue of humility, I would have to become a person which I wasn't. But the truth was that I misunderstood 'staying low' as giving up on my aliveness which I had as a child.

After contemplating the verse over and over again, I discovered something profound. I realised that Lao

Tzu wasn't asking me to give up on my expression or my aliveness; instead, he was asking me to stay low in the moments when I saw pride in myself. This realisation completely changed my perspective about how I should conduct myself and made me more mindful of traits such as pride and arrogance.

Soon, I started putting this verse into real-life practice. The first thing I noticed was that during meetings at work, I sometimes had an urge to just speak even when I did not have something substantial to say. I just wanted to speak in order to let people know about my presence. Another thing to note here is that moments of pride can be identified when in a conversation, you regularly use phrases such as 'I know', 'I am no less', and 'see I did it'. I started noticing that even though I did not say these sentences out loud, I did harbour them in my mind.

I immediately understood that all these acts were a symptom of pride in me. Reminding myself of the practice I was in, I started putting in the effort to quell my urge to speak at all times. I also started trying my best to remain silent and only speak when I had something significant to be say. This practice allowed me to really listen to my colleagues, understand their concerns and views, and approach them with mindful solutions when necessary. Consequently, people around me started listening to me keenly and the ideas I was proposing because now I too was listening to them. This practice also brought me a sense of ease and contentment as I could let go of the need to constantly make my presence felt and prove that I too am worthy. Now, I could be humble and lowly!

Take Aways

As we have already discussed, humility does not equate to being weak or powerless. Rather, it shows immense strength of character. As soon as the yearning for acknowledgement and admiration is relinquished, genuine connections with other beings begin to emerge. By embodying humility, you become akin to the valley of the world, where all rivers converge, as Lao Tzu expressed. I often recall the line 'staying low yet staying powerful' during moments of pride to remain grounded and mindful of the true essence of humility.

Bhagavad Gita also mentions humility as a pathway to realise true knowledge [13.8-12]:

> Humility, pridelessness, nonviolence, tolerance, simplicity, approaching a bona fide spiritual master, cleanliness, steadiness and self-control; renunciation of the objects of sense gratification, absence of false ego, the perception of the evil of birth, death, old age and disease; nonattachment to children, wife, home and the rest, and evenmindedness amid pleasant and unpleasant events; constant and unalloyed devotion to Me, resorting to solitary places, detachment from the general mass of people; accepting the importance of self-realization, and philosophical search for the Absolute Truth-all these I thus declare to be knowledge, and what is contrary to these is ignorance.

How to Practise Humility

Next time you find yourself in a situation where you feel the need to be noticed, respected, or recognised by the world, just take a pause and observe yourself—your body, your thoughts, and your emotions Recognise how this feeling restricts your ability to communicate effectively and constrains your potential to take the appropriate action in a certain area. By understanding the nature of these urges, you will be able to recognise them the next time they appear in you and handle them in a more mindful way. In case, doing all this might seem too difficult, you can write these scenarios in your journal and revisit them later. This way you can work on these areas one by one at a pace that works for you.

Chapter 15

Slowing Down

Do you feel as if you are trying to swim against the current of life? Do you find your daily life boring and mundane? If your answer is 'Yes' then you are not alone as the majority of us are stuck in a monotonous routine of waking up in the morning, doing the household chores, going to the office, coming back, eating, watching television, and then going to sleep. Not only that, but it also seems that we are always trying to catch up with life.

The simple truth behind why we feel so is that we are unable to live in the moment and instead, we are always waiting for the next thing—the next venture, the next trip, the next task, etc. This condition, which I call 'what's next', is exclusive to and widespread in human beings as no other creature suffers from it. All other living things are able to live from moment to moment, whereas we keep rushing for the next moment, trying to make the coming moment perfect. And in this process, the thing that we lose is the present moment.

Lao Tzu in several of his verses talks about the importance of stopping and slowing down in life and elaborates on the clarity and the harmony one experiences living in the present moment. Some of the verses that touched me are quoted below:

To keep on filling
is not as good as stopping.
Overfilled, the cupped hands drip,
better to stop pouring.

A contented man is never disappointed.
He who knows when to stop is preserved from
the peril,
Only thus can you endure long.

One who lives in accordance with nature,
Does not go against the way of things.
He moves in harmony with the present moment,
Always knowing the truth of just what to do.

Nowadays, it is very commonly seen that most of us live a hurried life. We do not have time to stop and slow down to experience the moment fully as we are always in a rush to complete the task at hand and get to the next thing. And not too long ago, my life mirrored this constant chase. Whether it was pursuing buses, rushing through metro stations, completing tasks in haste, or even trying to finish a meditation or exercise session quickly, I often found myself in pursuit of the next moment.

Certain verses from the earlier passages resonated deeply with me, especially the lines: 'Overfilled, the cupped hands drip; better to stop pouring.' These words served as a wake-up call, prompting me to realise that if I didn't halt this relentless chase and slow down, the cup of my life would inevitably drip dry. This insight compelled me to pause, appreciate the blessings in my life, and forge a stronger connection with nature.

I began to observe how elements of the natural world, such as trees, rivers, and birds, had the innate wisdom to slow down and savour the present moment. Watching ravens perched calmly on trees, even in the midst of rain, contrasted sharply with my own resistance when faced with discomfort. The birds became my silent teachers, imparting the value of stillness and presence in the face of adversity.

Incorporating this wisdom into my life, I made a conscious effort to slow down whenever I noticed myself rushing or attempting to control every aspect of my existence. A simple practice I adopted was to perform everyday tasks with grace and ease, as if I were caring for a delicate child. Cultivating gentleness allowed me to fully immerse myself in the present moment, leading to greater clarity in my actions.

An opportunity to put this practice into action presented itself one morning when I watched my bus pull away as I approached the stop. Despite the initial urge to sprint and catch it, I chose to continue walking with ease. This experience illuminated a profound truth: the way I began my day profoundly influenced the subsequent hours. Rushing and chasing led to a day filled with stress, whereas approaching tasks with ease and gentleness preserved inner peace.

Surprisingly, when I ceased running after buses and trains, they either halted for me or the next one arrived ahead of schedule. It became evident that when I acted with tranquillity, I never arrived late.

Take Aways

The most important take away from this chapter is that you are never truly late for anything; you are exactly where you're meant to be. Life unfolds in the present moment, not in the thoughts racing through your head or in some future moment. By cultivating a practice of presence, you open the doors to the entire universe.

So, take a deep breath and slow down. Allow that bus to pass you by on your way to the office or consider releasing that project you have been battling for months. You can even let go of that task that has been occupying your thoughts and preventing you from being in the moment. I am not suggesting irresponsibility or neglecting your commitments. What I am advocating is fulfilling your obligations with grace.

When you find yourself in a state of unease or discomfort, take a moment to pause. Stopping and dedicating just 10 minutes to relax won't cause you to miss deadlines, but it will undoubtedly help you restore your inner peace.

A beautiful quote on the importance of slowing down from the Roman stoic philosopher, Lucius Annaeus Seneca the Younger, commonly known as Seneca, goes as follows:

It does not matter how much time we are given if there is nowhere for it to settle; it escapes through the cracks and holes of the mind.

How to Practise the Art of Slowing Down

1. Make a declaration to yourself today that you will live this day with ease. Be attentive to moments when the impulse to rush and complete tasks swiftly arises. Also, be aware of the temptation to let your mind wander to future tasks while you are engaged in your current one. Recognise these urges, and consciously slow down. Approach your current task with gentleness. Infuse all your love and attention into the task at hand. Continuously monitor your inclination to jump ahead to the next task, acknowledge it, and then return to your current task, executing it with effortless grace. Repeat it aloud with unwavering confidence, 'I am choosing to be with this task in this moment.' By following this practice, you will rediscover the present moment in a fresh light and realise that being fully present opens up countless opportunities.
2. As a secondary exercise, make an effort to marvel at the small, everyday things in life. Pause to admire the blue sky, the graceful flight of a bird, raindrops delicately landing on leaves, the perfect drift of clouds, a bee

buzzing around flowers, the joyous laughter of children, the ceaseless chatter of a friend you might not always wish to hear, or even the concerns and worries expressed by your parents. If you take the time to slow down and observe these things, you will perceive a profound sense of perfection.

Chapter 16

Breaking Your Bondage

From the earliest moments of our existence, we are conditioned to seek validation and affirmation from those around us. The opinions of friends, family, and society at large become the metrics by which we measure our self-worth. As a result, we spend our entire lives in a perpetual quest for external validation and approval.

Here, what we need to realise is that liberation from these bondages and chains that hold us back lies in challenging the very foundations of this approval-seeking paradigm. Lao Tzu, in the verses of the Tao Te Ching, echoes this sentiment, asserting that the judgments of others can be the shackles that bind us.

The thirteenth verse of the Tao Te Ching eloquently highlights the perils of relentlessly pursuing or clinging to societal approval. This verse's essence implores us to transcend the judgments of others, whether they be wrapped in accolades or disdain, and to liberate ourselves from the chains of external validation.

Favour and disgrace seem alarming.
High status greatly afflicts your person.
Why are favour and disgrace alarming?
Seeking favour is degrading:
Alarming when it is gotten,
Alarming when it is lost.

Some time back, I found myself grappling with a sense of restraint when it came to saying 'No' to people.

With time, I have started enjoying a life of simplicity and finding solace in the tranquillity of nature rather than the company of others. My preferred sanctuary is amidst the natural world, where trees, forests, birds, and the gentle sunlight envelop me. However, I often judged myself harshly for desiring this solitude for extended periods. I felt guilty, thinking that by choosing to be alone, I was neglecting my responsibilities to others. This self-imposed obligation to constantly agree with others' desires, simply because I found it difficult to say no to them and express my own wishes started making me feel like I was in some form of captivity.

In the midst of this inner turmoil, I noticed that I was inclined to place blame on those around me, believing that they failed to comprehend or respect my choices. Then, one day, while walking by a farm, I observed animals enclosed by a fence. These creatures had convinced themselves that the fence was an insurmountable barrier, confining them for life. But upon closer inspection, I realised that the animals could easily leap over the fence; its height posed no true impediment. It made me ponder whether the bondage I felt in my own life was akin to that fence. Was it my own conviction that I couldn't cross this barrier, rather than the barrier itself, that held me back?

Something within me ignited, revealing that all forms of bondage are but illusions. They seem to exist, but in reality, they are not true barriers. It has always been me limiting myself. Hence, there is no bondage to break free from and no need to struggle. You and I can simply walk over these perceived limitations, for we are limitless, transcending beginnings and endings.

Therefore, it is crucial to introspect and ask yourself whether you are ensnared by the influence of others, or are you grappling with your own fear of appearing unfavourable or unkind. In my own journey, I discovered that it was exceptionally challenging for me to confront my actions when I believed they might cause harm or distress to others, as I empathise with the pain it can bring. This realisation unveiled the invisible thread that bound me to a particular persona in the presence of others. Since I had woven that thread myself, only I possessed the power to release it.

I came to understand that by relinquishing my attachment to preserving a specific image of being a kind person, I could sever the shackles of bondage. Furthermore, I realised that kindness does not always entail sugarcoating; it can manifest in clarity and directness. Over time, I began honing the art of saying 'No' with a harmonious blend of straightforwardness and transparency in my communication.

With this newfound understanding, I have embraced my choice to spend moments in silence. Some days, I choose to be with friends and family, while on others, I decline their invitations and express my need for solitude. And now that I have fully accepted this facet of myself, those around me have become more supportive and understanding. I have found complete freedom to be true to myself, and I am filled with profound appreciation for my loved ones, who not only understand me but also love me unconditionally.

Take Aways

The main take away of this chapter is that there has never been, nor will there ever be, any true bondage in your life. It is like that fence; it may appear to limit or impede you, but in reality, given your vastness and infinite nature, it can never truly constrain you. Refuse to buy into the illusion of any form of bondage, and recognise that you are an eternal, boundless being. Understand that all forms of restraint are mere illusions. You alone have the power to restrict or liberate yourself, for you are the architect of your own reality. Your words, creations, and beliefs shape the world in which you dwell.

The profound exploration of the concept of bondage can also be found in the pages of the book *Yoga Vasistha*. This text documents a dialogue between Sage Vasistha and Prince Rama when the latter seeks the sage's guidance. Within its pages, Sage Vasistha engages in a discourse with Prince Rama, delving into the notions of bondage and liberation. He emphasises that our own thoughts and beliefs serve as the self-imposed barriers in our lives and, therefore, none of them exist independently.

First destroy the mental conditioning by renouncing cravings; and then remove from your mind even the concept of bondage and liberation. Be totally free of conditioning. Ideas and thoughts are bondage; and their coming to an end is liberation. Therefore, be free of them and do whatever has to be done spontaneously. (III:111)

How to Practise Going beyond Your Limitations

1. Observe your reactions when someone instructs you to do something, and you respond with a 'No'. What unfolds within you? Do you find inner peace after declining the request, or do you grapple with frustration and confusion, pondering why people place such expectations on you? Reflect on why their reactions weigh on you, and why it disturbs you to assert your own desires. Is it their disappointment or your desire to conform that binds you? In this introspective moment, identify the true source of your constraints.
2. As an additional exercise, compile a list of your 'Have Tos' in life—those obligations you believe you must fulfil without alternative. Delve into each one, examining what keeps you bound to these obligations. Take them one by one, and inquire: Is it external pressures or my own internal beliefs that restrict me? What mental constructs hold me captive, and

how can I foster freedom in these areas? The act of contemplation itself initiates the process of self-discovery. Embrace these questions with patience and compassion, knowing that answers will reveal themselves when the time is right.

Chapter 17

Forests—My Eternal Partner

The mere mention of the word 'forest' brings a smile to my face. The towering, magnificent trees, the vibrant green surroundings, the melodic chirping of birds, and the abundance of flora and fauna that thrives in this enchanting place make it truly exceptional and captivating.

One of the aspects I adore about the forest is its unabashed authenticity. It confidently embraces its true nature without any shame, guilt, or blame. Also, similar to human beings, forests undergo numerous transformations throughout their lifecycle, but what continually captivates me is their remarkable ability to exude beauty through every change. It's as if the forest's very existence is a testament to embracing the natural flow of change, enhancing its allure. In fact, it is the very change that enhances its beauty even more.

In the pages of Tao Te Ching, Lao Tzu frequently draws our attention to the wonders of nature, encouraging us to observe and glean wisdom from the natural world.

The sixty-sixth verse teaches us about being like the sea:

> Why is the sea king of a hundred streams?
> Because it lies below them.
> Humility gives it its power.

The seventy-sixth verse beseeches us to be flexible and alive like the grass and trees:

> A man is born gentle and weak;
> At his death he is hard and stiff.
> All things, including the grass and trees,
> Are soft and pliable in life;
> Dry and brittle in death.

Out of the many virtues forests have taught me, one of them is flexibility. Trees are epitomes of adaptability as they always find a way to flourish despite obstacles. The forests' capacity to adjust to each season, all while retaining their beauty, never fails to inspire awe.

Flexibility—it is a word that resonates with all of us. We aspire to be flexible, to flow like a river effortlessly. No one desires rigidity, for it often leaves us feeling stuck, resulting in inner tension and stiffness that we project onto others.

Yet, the real test arises when we sense rigidity creeping within us, when we become entrenched in our own viewpoints. Is it feasible to release our convictions and embrace flexibility during such moments? I would assert that it is indeed possible, but only if we genuinely desire it. Otherwise, the process remains difficult.

With a genuine desire to embody this virtue, the universe presented me with a challenging test, one where I struggled to let go of my own self-righteousness.

Some time ago, a few friends visited my home, and I was excited to meet them. However, as they settled in, I began to feel increasingly uncomfortable. As always, I started looking into why I was feeling these emotions, leading me to uncover several reasons behind my unease. I have a penchant for orderliness in my home, including setting up my kitchen, cleaning the house, putting everything in its place before I sleep, feeding my cat exactly the right amount he is supposed to eat, and following my morning routine. However, my daily life took a different turn when my friends arrived. There was a lot of disorder in the house as we were cooking together, and the house became quite unclean very quickly. It became evident how attached I was to cleanliness and the immediate restoration of order when things didn't align with my preferences.

I typically practice open and loving communication to address issues that trigger upsetting emotions within me. I also listen with empathy to understand the perspectives of others, seeking fresh possibilities. However, during this period, something was amiss, and I found myself frequently angry and upset. I realised that this was because I was accustomed to doing things at my home in my own way, on my own schedule, and when this routine changed, I did not like it. It was here that I recognised an opportunity to embody the qualities of a tree—flexible and humble, yet strong and unwavering.

I began to question the utility of my spiritual practices if I couldn't cultivate flexibility within myself. Even when my ideas appeared 'nice' or aligned with my vision of a happy and peaceful life, I pondered their worth if they led to inflexibility. This challenge was particularly daunting because I had what I considered a 'valid' reason for my frustrations. However, I recognised that these difficulties were, in fact, the Tao's way of teaching me to be adaptable and pliant.

Gradually, I let go of my rigid insistence on doing things a certain way, and I noticed a remarkable reduction in the significance of my irritations. While I continued to restore order in the house, I did so without experiencing emotional turmoil. And as I did this, I began to appreciate the many ways my friends were contributing to the upkeep of the house, which I had previously overlooked. My anger and frustrations had blinded me to their positive efforts. My perspective underwent a transformation, and I observed my friends diligently tending to my house and kitchen exactly as I preferred. Embracing flexibility and incorporating their approaches into my own way of doing things created an environment where diverse methods coexisted harmoniously.

Once again, the forests, my eternal companions, imparted yet another lesson on how to radiate love to everyone around me.

Take Aways

Be like the forests, all-embracing, open, and receptive. Just as the forest welcomes all within its embrace while safeguarding its own essence, it gracefully adapts to the ever-changing tides of transformation.

Consider this: If trees lacked flexibility, could they ever find room for growth? It is the forest's inherent capacity to bend when necessary, that allows it to thrive even in the harshest conditions. On your inner journey, be prepared, much like the forest, to relinquish your preconceived notions and beliefs. Sometimes, these ideas may seem incredibly 'useful', 'pleasant', or 'meditative'. However, any idea or concept that limits you should be given up. These ideas exist to support you and not to block you from expanding into the totality of the being you are!

Albert Einstein, a preeminent physicist of the twentieth century, once shared his reflections on nature:

> Look deep into the nature, and then you will understand everything better.

How to Be Like Forests

To be like forests, immerse yourself in their presence. If access to a forest isn't readily available, spending time in a park or any natural setting with trees will suffice.

Begin by closely observing the intricate details: the lush green leaves, the vibrant array of flowers in hues of pink, yellow, and blue, the sturdy bark of trees, and the way they reach out to one another. Develop a deep appreciation for these remarkable beings, which not only provide us protection but also enrich our lives in more ways than one.

Take a moment to gently touch some leaves and flowers, feeling their textures, and recognise their vulnerability and fragility, yet their enduring beauty and strength. Notice the similarities between their characteristics and those of our own bodies.

Reflect on how you can cultivate these qualities within yourself—being humble like the sea and flexible like the trees. Through silent observation and breathing along with the forest, you can unravel many of the mysteries of life. I often get a lot of my answers when I get up early in the morning and go out to meet my eternal partner: the forest.

Chapter 18

Clarity amidst Chaos

Chaos, well the word itself, introduces a feeling of disorder within us. Chaos often manifests when elements or situations in your life descend into complete disarray. It can arise when life unfolds at a pace that feels uncomfortable or when everything you wish to avoid seems to present itself in your life.

Thus, we can see that chaos can show up in different forms and at different times. During such tumultuous times, it becomes imperative to turn inward. Self-inquiry is a powerful tool for introspection, allowing you to delve into your inner self and gain understanding. It is through self-awareness that chaos can ultimately transform into clarity.

Lao Tzu, in the thirty-third verse, shares the importance of knowing oneself.

> One who understands others has knowledge,
> One who understands himself has wisdom.
> Mastering others requires force,
> Mastering the self needs strength.

Carrying this verse of wisdom from Lao Tzu in my heart, I soon encountered a situation where I could put his teachings into practice.

Not too long ago, two of my closest friends visited my home for a get-together, and during our time together, a heated argument erupted between them. It escalated to the point where physical intervention was necessary to defuse the situation.

I found myself drained of energy and uncertain about how to handle the situation. Whenever I tried to mediate between my friends, they perceived bias, leaving me caught in the middle. The chaos and misunderstandings among them took a toll on my own well-being, inducing anxiety. Yet, the wisdom of the Tao gently nudged me to turn inward for self-inquiry.

I began to question my discomfort: Why was I so eager to resolve this situation hastily? The answer emerged—I craved peace and harmony for myself. I yearned to restore order because I couldn't tolerate the chaos. But was the chaos solely external, or did it also dwell within me? I realised that my urge to hurriedly fix the situation was fueling this inner turmoil. Moreover, this impulse was driven solely by my desire to regain personal tranquillity, with little regard for the well-being of those embroiled in the conflict.

With these questions in my heart, I decided to step back from the situation. I ceased justifying or explaining matters to either friend. Instead, I assessed what needed to be done to conclude the gathering and took care of it. I released all attachments and expectations regarding how my friends should behave, acknowledging them as individuals with free will. I granted them the space to reflect on the situation. By disengaging from personal interests and desires, I observed that a few days later, they began conversing with each other once more.

Through this process of introspection and turning inward, the chaos within me transformed into absolute clarity. Ultimately, I no longer felt shaken or uncertain.

Take Aways

Every bit of chaos that we experience in our physical world can be seen as events happening in time and space. And it is us who give these events meaning. If we could see these events without pasting our own created meanings, then we can see the reality for what it actually is. The fact is that most of our issues will dissolve when we start seeing things as they are.

Another important point to remember is that the chaos you experience outside is just a reflection of what is happening inside of you. This means that by just turning inside and uncovering what is happening inside of you, you can accordingly transform your external situation from being chaotic to tranquil. And once chaos subsides, clarity shows up.

Lastly, we also need to view chaos correctly. We often associate disorder with chaos and order with clarity. It is only in the space of total chaos that one can experience total clarity. Thus, we can say that clarity doesn't exist independent of chaos; rather, it emerges from chaos.

Numerous ancient texts emphasise the significance of self-inquiry. Yoga Vasistha mentions the significance of looking inside oneself as exemplified by Sage Vasistha's responses to Prince Rama's inquiries about the four gatekeepers to freedom.

> They in whom the spirit of inquiry is ever awake illumine the world, enlighten all who come into contact with them, dispel the ghosts created by an ignorant mind, and realise the falsity of sense-pleasures and their objects. O' Rama, in the light of inquiry there is realisation of the eternal and unchanging reality; this is the supreme. With it one does not long for any other gain nor does one spurn anything. He is free from delusion, attachment; he is not inactive nor does he get drowned in action; he lives and functions in this world and at the end of a natural life-span he reaches the blissful state of total freedom. The eye of spiritual inquiry does not lose its sight even in the midst of all activities.

Patanjali's *Yoga Sutras* are also filled with verses on self-enquiry.

> When the mind is disturbed by improper thoughts, constant pondering over the opposites is the remedy. [2:33]

How to Generate Clarity amidst Chaos

1. Spend some time writing in your journal about what chaos means to you and some instances in the past when you encountered chaotic situations. Also, write down your emotional

reactions to these scenarios, delving into the feelings that arose during those moments.

Following that, articulate what clarity signifies to you and describe the emotions you experience when clarity emerges in your life. By recognising and distinguishing between these feelings, you can enhance your self-awareness and gain the skills to identify and effectively manage such emotions in the future.

2. Begin by paying attention to any chaotic situations that arise in your life from today onward. Simply observe how you feel when you're in these situations. Your awareness alone can sometimes bring about significant changes. In the midst of these situations, continue to fulfil your responsibilities as required.

   Later, take time to reflect on the emotions that arise within you during these moments of chaos. If there are issues that can be addressed or communicated, approach them with love rather than blame, and express the thoughts and feelings you have been holding back. If there is nothing to address, practice acceptance and embrace the situations as they are. Worrying will not resolve your issues, so let go of unnecessary concern. Throughout this process, be gentle and kind to yourself. Contemplating these questions and listening to your inner self can bring clarity to your life.

Chapter 19

Accepting All of Me

Like everyone else, there are many sides to me as well. There is the angry me, the empathetic me, the sad me, the joyous me, the irritated me, and the content me, just to name a few. And sometimes, I would switch from one version of myself to another in a moment.

But one thing I noticed was that there were some versions of me that I liked and some that I did not. In other words, I wanted myself to be a certain way and expunge parts of me which I felt weren't good enough. Due to this division, I suffered and experienced conflicting emotions inside of me. I saw that I often accepted myself when I performed well or when I operated as per the 'rules of the society' while it was hard for me to accept myself when I was angry, confused, or in a state that wasn't considered ideal by the people.

One day, I came across the second verse of the Tao Te Ching which gave me an edifying insight into the importance of embracing all parts of me. It read as follows:

> Being and non-being give birth to each other,
> Difficult and easy accomplish each other,
> Long and short form each other
> High and low distinguish each other
> Sound and tone harmonise each other
> Before and after follow each other
> Realising this, the saint performs effortlessly according to the natural way without personal desire, and practices the wordless teaching through one's deeds.

This verse explores the aspect of duality or polarities experienced by human beings. And these polarities are not just mental constructs but also make up our physical realities. For example, we can only distinguish long hair if we know the concept of short hair.

This concept has also been mentioned in other ancient philosophies. In the Chinese tradition, we have a concept of *yin yang* which represents the connection and dependency between the complementary states, each contributing itself to the emergence and fall of the other. In other words, one is required for the other to be there.

For us to accept ourselves fully, it is important to understand the nature of these polarities rising and falling in us. Therefore, in an attempt to practice this verse, I developed a habit of pausing whenever I experienced anger or any other uncomfortable emotion surging within me. During these moments, I closely observed the emergence of these emotions and became attuned to how they manifested in various parts of my body, such as my chest, throat, and stomach. This heightened awareness allowed me to discern the intricate interplay among these conflicting emotions, as they influenced each other's rise and fall.

I came to realise that much like the ever-changing weather on our planet, the emotional climate within me was in constant flux. Yet, I understood that each emotional season was necessary. Just as the presence of winter paves the way for spring, these emotional states create conditions for one another to coexist and evolve.

I ultimately recognised that all these states and versions of myself were essential in shaping my current reality. Once I perceived these variations as blessings, it became much easier for me to embrace and accept all aspects of my being.

Therefore, practising this verse and imbibing its core insight allowed me to accept all the aspects of myself that I liked and disliked. I realised that there is no bad or good, right or wrong. And therefore, the idea of accepting or rejecting certain parts of me became redundant as they weren't separate things. In fact, nothing in this life can exist on its own and requires everything else for it to be there. This realisation opened up a whole new world for me. I became comfortable with all sides of me and conflicting emotions within me subsided. I let go of all the judgements that I carried against myself. Not only that, but I also became more accepting of others and all their versions.

Take Aways

The all of me and the all of you are so diverse and different that it is natural to cling on to the versions which we are familiar with and find pleasant and avoid the ones which are unpleasant. But as the Tao states, the concept of long cannot exist without its counterpart, the short. Similarly, in order for us to achieve wholeness, we must fully accept and embrace every emotion that arises within us, regardless of whether it is pleasant or unpleasant. If you can sit patiently and observe how the different versions of yourself rise and fall in you, you will soon discover that all of these states are transient. The interplay of polarities inherent within us can be found in the natural world around us, where the rain facilitates the radiance of the sun, and conversely, the sun allows the rain to descend upon us. Each element relies on the other's presence, emphasising their interconnectedness. Clinging to one version of ourselves and repelling others only causes suffering as all these versions are impermanent. This insight can help us disassociate with the emotions and states that rise and fall in us. With this realisation, we can naturally engage in actions that align with our inherent purpose in life.

A beautiful excerpt from the book, *No Mud, No Lotus*, elaborates on the significance of self-acceptance and self-love.

> Both suffering and happiness are of an organic nature, which means they are both transitory; they are always changing. The flower, when it

wilts, becomes the compost. The compost can help grow a flower again. Happiness is also organic and impermanent by nature. It can become suffering and suffering can become happiness again.

How to Practise Self-Acceptance

1. The next time you find yourself grappling with uncomfortable emotions, take a moment to step back and watch these emotions as they emerge and subside within you. Tune into the physical sensations associated with these emotions. Observe how one emotion seamlessly transitions into another, often within a matter of hours. Keep a record of your reflections and insights in your journal.
2. Embrace the natural flow of life. Rather than pushing away or magnifying particular facets of yourself or your emotional states, simply live with simplicity and authenticity. Engage in work when it's necessary and allow yourself to relax when relaxation is called for.

Chapter 20

You Are Important

Human beings have a clear purpose—to contribute. This was one of the lines that once my coach said to me, and at the time, I didn't understand what it meant. However, later in my life, the universe imparted this wisdom to me that everything we encounter in the physical world, every being we observe, contributes to one another in some way. This implies that each of us holds significance and worthiness.

Yet, there are moments in life when we feel undesired, insignificant, or unworthy. Have you pondered the reasons behind such feelings and questioned what truly defines our importance and worthiness? Is it our titles, positions, qualifications, or social standing? Or could it be something entirely different? Before we explore this, allow me to share some lines from the thirty-ninth verse of the Tao Te Ching that deeply resonated with me in this context:

The sky is whole and clear
The earth is whole and firm.

The spirit is whole and full.
The 10,000 things are whole, and the country is upright.
All these are in virtue of wholeness.

The pieces of a chariot are useless unless they work in accordance with the whole.
A man's life brings nothing unless he lives in accordance with the whole universe.
Playing one's part in accordance with the universe is true humility.

This verse beautifully emphasises the notion that everything emanating from the same source is inherently whole, which includes all of us, as we too originated from that source. These lines helped me in a situation when I was doubting my self-worth at work. This was during the time I had just joined a new team at my work. My colleagues were quite outstanding at what they did and had qualifications and degrees from the top universities in the world. On the other hand, I, who just moved from another country, had a lot of inferiority complexes as I believed my qualifications and degrees didn't measure up to those of my colleagues. I then noticed a recurring tendency in myself where I would frequently engage in comparing my abilities and accomplishments with those of my colleagues, leading to feelings of inadequacy and a sense of not fitting in within the team.

My inner turmoil intensified because I was also well aware of Lao Tzu's wisdom that 'All of us are whole, and everyone is supposed to play their part in this universe.' This knowledge created a constant conflict within me.

There would be moments when I felt utterly unworthy, and then there were times when I grappled with guilt for my inability to fully embrace Lao Tzu's wisdom. Failing to find a resolution, I eventually found myself with no alternative but to embark on a profound journey of self-contemplation to address this internal conflict.

After grappling with this conflict for some time, to my surprise, it was a simple encounter with a small bee that helped to resolve this issue. While out in a park, I observed a bee firmly grasping onto a flower, and the flower remained completely receptive to the bee's presence. In that very moment, a sudden awakening happened in me, and I recognised how the bee contributed to the flower through the process of pollination, while the flower reciprocated by offering its nectar. At that instant, the words of my coach made complete sense to me, that indeed, we all exist for the purpose of contribution. I became acutely aware that even small entities like a bee and a flower possess intrinsic importance and play their unique roles in the universe, which have a far-reaching impact on life on our planet. I also realised that if the bee and the flower ceased their vital roles, life as we know it would not be sustained.

I then wondered, 'Then how can I not be important?' I became aware of the fact that I too have my unique gifts to offer, and they may not be the same as other people in my team but still have their part of contribution to my team. The next day when I arrived at work, I could see myself and my team with a fresh perspective. The feeling of unworthiness and inadequacy gently faded away and I felt myself bonding more with my team members.

Take Aways

Every entity in this universe, whether it's you, me, the mountains, the sky, or the animals, is inherently whole and complete. We all share a common origin from the same source, the Tao, which in itself is whole and unbroken. Our existence is interconnected, and we contribute to the grand tapestry of life in ways that might not always be immediately evident. Yet, with patience and close observation, we can uncover our importance in this intricate chain of existence.

It is essential to recognise that every action you take carries significant consequences for the entire planet. Your mere presence reverberates throughout the cosmos. If you were in any way 'useless', you wouldn't exist in the first place.

One of the classic examples that you can see around you and inside you right now, is how you and the microbes in your body are contributing to each other at this very moment as well! There are trillions of microbes working for you at this moment so that you can have a proper digestion and generate vitamins necessary for your healthy body. At the same time, you are contributing to these microbes for their growth. Every life on our planet home that you can see is wanted and important and has a purpose constantly contributing to one form or the other!

How to Work on Self-Worth

1. To nurture your sense of self-worth, begin by identifying the areas in your life where you experience a lack of it. Open your journal and jot down instances when you have felt small or unworthy, especially in the company of certain people or under particular circumstances. Try to understand what triggers these feelings of diminished self-importance. Avoid getting caught in a cycle of blame, where you attribute these feelings solely to others, as this can perpetuate the cycle of negativity. Instead, focus on recognising and becoming aware of these areas within yourself.
2. Carrying the wisdom of Lao Tzu in your heart, take some time today to observe the often overlooked contributions that everyone, including yourself, makes in the grand scheme of this planet. If it's challenging to see this in human interactions, begin by observing the contributions of beings in nature. Choose the path of least resistance to start shifting your perspective.
3. In your journal, record instances where you feel you have made a positive impact on someone's life in recent weeks. This exercise serves as a form of self-acknowledgement, where you take a moment to recognise the remarkable aspects of yourself and commend your own contributions.

By quietly observing yourself and others as integral parts of the grand universe, you will gradually come to understand that all forms of life hold significance on this planet, including you.

Chapter 21
Embracing Death

What's your reaction when you think about death? Are you overcome by fear when you think about the death of a loved one? Do you try to block such thoughts and avoid thinking about death completely?

Death and birth are universal phenomena, and they are happening at all times, whether we are aware of it or not. Every day, countless living things take birth while many return back to the source through death. And these phenomena take place on every level. Even at the cellular level, each day, millions of cells in our body die to make way for new ones.

And even after the ubiquitousness of these phenomena and knowing the fact that they are intertwined, we don't view them equally. We embrace birth and resist death. In fact, death remains a taboo subject and when faced with it, people either turn to things they believe will shield them from it or ignore it completely.

The fiftieth verse of the Tao Te Ching presents death in a lucid and profound manner:

Between birth and death, three in ten are followers of life;
three in ten are followers of death.
And men just passing from birth to death also number three in ten.
Why is this so?
Because they clutch to life and cling to this passing world.
But there is one out of ten, they say, so sure of life that tigers and wild bulls keep clear.
Weapons turn from him on the battlefield,
rhinoceroses have no place to horn him,
tigers find no place for claws, and
soldiers have no place to thrust their blades.
Why is this so?
Because he dwells in that place where death cannot enter.
Realise your essence and you will witness the end without ending.

I personally had to grapple with the concept of death and how it relates to us during the coronavirus pandemic. When the first wave hit India, the number of hospitalisations drastically increased and due to the limited availability of beds, many people died simply because they could not get a bed in a hospital. Hotel rooms and other such spaces were converted into makeshift hospitals by the government, but these measures were not enough as the number of cases was too overwhelming. The situation was made even worse by the fact that this variant was specifically hitting the respiratory systems of people, causing an immediate drop in oxygen levels, and the scarcity of oxygen cylinders added to the death toll in the country.

It was during this time I found that my parents had gotten infected by the virus. Since I was in a different country, I initially had a lot of anxiety and panic when I got to know about the condition of my parents. I and my family members worked together to arrange the medicines and other requisites to bring them into a stable state. Luckily, my father recovered after a couple of days, but the condition of my mother kept on deteriorating. I was unable to sleep for several nights. I spent each moment dreading that I would anytime get the news that my mother had passed away.

I spoke to many doctors over the phone, and they prescribed a lot of medicines for my mother. However, my mother had an issue with taking so many medicines. She kept saying to me that she was not comfortable having the medicines in such large quantities, but I was too scared about her health and asked her to follow the prescription provided by the doctor. But this was to no avail as her condition didn't improve.

Then one of the doctors prescribed a specific medicine which we weren't able to find even after repeated attempts. The fact that I was unable to arrange this medicine for my mother really broke me. I remember that it was tulips season, and I was standing in front of a patch of tulips, helplessly crying out for help. Standing next to the flower field, I asked them to support me in finding the medicine we all were seeking. It was this time when the Tao manifested as the flowers in front of me and spoke back to me. I heard something inside of me, 'Maybe your mother doesn't need what you are seeking. Maybe she needs something else.'

At that moment, I paused to observe what I had been doing and what I realised shook me to my core. I realised that I was so afraid of losing my mother that I wasn't even listening to what she wanted. And due to my fear of 'she might leave us', I was asking her to pop 30-40 pills a day. The fact of the matter was that this whole thing was about me and not her as I was unsure about what will I do without her. I also realised that no medicine, doctor, or hospital could do anything if my mother chose to leave us.

Realising this, I completely broke down and tears started rolling down my cheeks. I knew that I had to stop trying to control things and allow the course of events to happen. This epiphany also completely changed my perception of death. It was no longer an antagonist who we need to fight relentlessly but rather an important part of life that we should accept when it arrives.

I then called my mother and asked her, 'What will bring you to ease? Do that. Listen and trust your body and see what it wants.' It was difficult for me to let go of this control because I believed if I didn't take action, my mother would leave us. And in this process of trying to control everything, I took away the freedom of my parents to take decisions about their lives. The truth was that I had forgotten that I wasn't the one running the universe.

And when I let go of my fear of losing my mother and gave her the choice to do what she found the best for her health, we all created a new possibility of getting a second opinion from another doctor. And as life would have it, the new doctor prescribed fewer medicines to my mother and soon, she recovered.

Take Away

Death is an inevitable part of life, yet we find it difficult to consider and confront the topic of death. We would rather sweep it under the carpet and live our lives as if there is no end to it. But no matter how much we try to ignore it, it is sure to make its presence felt in one way or the other, especially when a loved one passes away. Thus, it is imperative to establish a relationship with ourselves and others that goes beyond death.

And this is what Lao Tzu is trying to teach us. He is saying that if we release our clutch on life, then death cannot take anything from us as there will be nothing to take away in the first place. And this is only possible if we realise our true essence which transcends our body and mind.

A beautiful song from the book, *No Death, No Fear,* written by the Vietnamese monk, Thich Nhat Hanh, also elucidates this idea.

> This body is not me; I am not caught in this body, I am life without boundaries, I have never been born and I have never died. Over there the wide ocean and the sky with many galaxies; All manifest from the basis of consciousness. Since beginningless time I have always been free. Birth and death are only a door through which we go in and out. Birth and death are only a game of hide-and-seek. So smile to me and take my hand and wave goodbye. Tomorrow we shall meet again

or even before. We shall always be meeting again at the true source, always meeting again on the myriad paths of life.

How to Practise Death-Acceptance

1. Take some time out and sit in front of a mirror.
2. Look into your eyes and silently ask:
    - Who am I beyond this body?
    - Where is this energy coming from that allows me to move my hand, speak, walk, and run?
    - What is the origin of this voice that grants me the ability to express myself and communicate with others?
    - Am I in any way involved in this phenomenon?
    - If my body decides to cease functioning today, do I possess any power to influence it?
3. Write down your answers to these questions in your journal and contemplate them.

Once you start doing this exercise regularly, the fear of death will start diminishing as you will find yourself to be part of an infinite energy that has given all of us an opportunity to live, thrive, and work. You will realise that birth and death are two facets in the play of this infinite energy.

And though it might feel as if we are doing things, the truth is that it is this infinite energy that is doing things through us. And when death arrives, we will just leave our physical bodies but continue to be a part of this energy.

Chapter 22

Choice—The Source of Confusion

The act of making a choice has many aspects to it. Sometimes, having a range of options can be exhilarating, brimming with possibilities and abundance. On other occasions, however, it can lead to confusion. Whether it is the little decisions like selecting a red dress over a white one or the major life-altering choices such as picking between job offers from different companies or even choosing a life partner. In short, choices can be exciting as well as a source of confusion in our lives.

But have you ever wondered why choices can lead to confusion and even anxiety? Why do we find ourselves in states of uncertainty and hesitation when faced with choices? What do we stand to lose by choosing one path over another? Should we conform to societal expectations and make 'safe' choices, even when they don't align with our true desires?

Despite the struggles and inner turmoil involved when it comes to decision-making, we ultimately make our choices. So, the important question to consider here is whether it's possible to make choices in life with a sense of freedom and if so, what does it truly mean to choose with freedom?

I believe that choosing with freedom involves being fully aware of the potential consequences of our choices in life and yet making those choices with power and conviction, devoid of fear or unrealistic hopes. Many times, when we make a choice, we do so with thoughts like, 'I hope everything turns out well', 'I hope I am making the right decision', or 'I hope I am not making a mistake'. Such inner dialogues breed uncertainty, fear, and doubt regarding our choices. In such a state, we are not truly free; we are bound by apprehensions and anxieties about the potential outcomes. Choosing with freedom entails letting go of the fear of making the 'wrong' choice. We should stand in a place where we can embrace the consequences of our choices, recognising that there is no definitive right or wrong choice. What we need to realise is that a choice is simply a choice, and it comes with its own set of outcomes, whether we make it or not.

A few lines from the twentieth verse of the Tao Te Ching that profoundly resonated with me have been shared below:

What is the difference between yes and no?
What is the difference between good and evil?

Must I fear what others fear from?
Should I fear desolation
When there is abundance?

Should I fear darkness
When that light is shining everywhere?

Some time back, I found myself facing a dilemma where I had to choose between a 'yes' or 'no' in response to a long-standing question in my life. I was striving to make the right choice while grappling with considerable confusion on multiple fronts. But is there truly a difference between a 'yes' or a 'no'?

My husband and I have had a wonderful relationship which we cherish deeply. However, I often did not feel a strong desire to have children. When I saw other women of my age raising children, I used to get into doubt and fear. Doubt about whether I was making the right decision, if my choice was the 'correct' one, or if I would come to regret it later in life. For some time, I didn't realise but I was consistently judging myself for not having a desire to have children. Also, the idea of talking to someone about the fact that I wasn't looking to have children as of now was very uncomfortable for me. This was because I knew that they wouldn't fully understand from where my decision was arising. This was until I embarked on a journey of reading the verses of the Tao.

One day, I dedicated some time to deep contemplation, delving into the feelings of inner conflict that had been troubling me when it came to motherhood. Upon close examination, I came to a startling realisation that this confusion was a product of my own making. It was a carefully constructed mental fog, a strategy I employed to evade responsibility for my actions and choices. When I allowed myself to dwell in this confusion, I found solace in the notion that I could better justify my decisions, even if they were deemed wrong.

Then, while strolling home from work one day, I had a vision of the future. This vision showed me two paths—one where I saw myself as a mother, and the other one where I wasn't a mother. Astonishingly, both scenarios filled me with profound bliss and fulfilment. I felt complete and at peace no matter the scenario in my vision.

And then I heard a voice inside of me that said that there was no wrong choice! Every decision carries its own set of challenges, but your fulfilment is independent of the choice itself. Regardless of the path you choose, you can create a sense of fulfilment and happiness. At that moment, I realised that the light of contentment and joy shines perpetually, and it's up to me whether or not I want to tap into it. At that moment, I remembered Lao Tzu's words: 'Should I fear desolation when that abundant energy is everywhere?'

This revelation brought me a sense of inner serenity and the understanding that there was no wrong choice, only choices with their respective consequences. Moreover, this insight shed light on my procrastination regarding a decision about my health, specifically whether or not to undergo a molar extraction. It also revealed a similar pattern at my workplace, where I was uncertain about changing jobs.

In all these instances, I had mistakenly believed that external circumstances or the people in my life were the sources of my confusion. In reality, I had created this confusion as a shield against taking responsibility for my choices, all due to my fear of making wrong or bad decisions. Ultimately, I realised that there are no right or wrong choices and that there is no sure shot way to be certain about the choices in life. The only thing we can do is have faith in ourselves and choose a path which we believe in.

Kindly note that the context of this chapter is not to advocate for or against having children. Instead, it aims to empower individuals to make their life choices with confidence and clarity.

Take Aways

The key takeaway here is that there is no definitive right or wrong choice. Regardless of how much time you invest in evaluating the pros and cons of a decision, you ultimately need to select one option from the myriad of possibilities in your life. I am not suggesting that one should disregard practical considerations or ignore the advantages and disadvantages associated with a choice—indeed, it is wise to consider these factors. However, what I am proposing is to embrace a state of being. To be powerful and fully receptive to the consequences that your choice will entail. To be aware, while making a choice, that the choice itself has limited influence over your overall fulfilment and happiness. Each choice will undoubtedly present its own set of challenges, which may contribute to your fulfilment or happiness, but the true source of your fulfilment and happiness is always you. It doesn't depend on external circumstances or possessions.

I really resonated with the following lines from the book, *The Book of Secrets: Unlocking the Hidden Dimensions of Your Life*, written by Deepak Chopra:

If you obsess over whether you are making the right decision, you are basically assuming that the universe will reward you for one thing and punish you for another. The universe has no fixed agenda. Once you make any decision, it works around that decision. There is no right or wrong, only a series of possibilities that shift with each thought, feeling, and action that you experience.

If this sounds too mystical, refer again to the body. Every significant vital sign—body temperature, heart rate, oxygen consumption, hormone level, brain activity, and so on—alters the moment you decide to do anything . . . decisions are signals telling your body, mind, and environment to move in a certain direction.

How to Choose Freedom

1. To engage with the concepts discussed in this chapter, take a moment today to identify all the areas in your life where you find yourself confused and unsure. These are situations where you need to take action but have been hesitant due to your sense of bewilderment.
2. Now, for each of these areas, ask yourself what is holding you back from taking action, especially when you already know the pros and cons of each choice. You will find that it is often the fear of not making the right choice that holds you back from making a choice.

3. To get clarity on the matter, write down what works for you and what does not work for you in each of the choices and use these insights to support your decision-making process. Trust yourself as you inherently know what's right for you. Trust that knowledge and make your choice. And regardless of the choice you make and the path you select, remember that you are the source of your own fulfilment and happiness. It's not the circumstances or outcomes stemming from your choices that determine your fulfilment and happiness. With this awareness, make your choices freely, recognising that you are the driving force in your life and not the consequences of your choice!

Chapter 23

The Absolute Truth

Since time immemorial, the human species has been involved in the quest for truth. This is due to the fact that it is our nature to seek, and we have been long seeking the deepest secrets of life and everything it entails. But what is the truth and how does it relate to each one of us?

Simply put, truth is a fact or a belief that is accepted as true. Based on this definition, I believe that truth can be multifarious and that everyone has their own version of the truth. Meaning, there could be something that you believe to be true but might not be true for the other person.

There is also a drawback when we regard something as the absolute truth, and that being is that it prevents us from seeing or considering anything else that can be the truth. Since we all keep supporting our own versions of the truth, sometimes we lose respect for the truth of the other person. This can limit our ability to remain open to other aspects of the same conversation, as well as our capacity to embrace or coexist with a person with conflicting ideas.

The fifty-second verse of the Tao eloquently captures this absolute truth, which gave birth to everything:

> In the beginning was the Tao.
> All things issue from it;
> all things return to it.
>
> To find the origin,
> trace back the manifestations.
> When you recognize the children
> and find the mother,
> you will be free of sorrow.
>
> If you close your mind in judgements
> and traffic with desires,
> your heart will be troubled.
> If you keep your mind from judging
> and aren't led by the senses,
> your heart will find peace.
>
> Seeing into darkness is clarity.
> Knowing how to yield is strength.
> Use your own light
> and return to the source of light.
> This is called practicing eternity.

Over time, as I immersed myself in the verses of the Tao, I began to develop my own set of spiritual practices. I diligently followed these practices day in and day out. For example, one of my practices involved getting up early in the morning for meditation. However, if there were days when I overslept and didn't adhere to my practices, I would feel a sense of discomfort. It felt as though I had become confined by my own practices. I didn't realise it at the time, but I started to believe that the practices I was engaged in were the sole truth and the only correct path to leading a fulfilling life. This belief closed me off from considering other practices that people around me were following.

Looking back, I can see that I had become rigid in my commitment to my own practices. Whenever rigidity takes hold, it can create a sense of stagnation within and around us. Recognising my own sense of being stuck, I realised that I had developed a strong sense of righteousness about my own practices, as if they were the ultimate truth in the world or the only path to follow in the journey of transformation. This realisation made me more receptive to the diverse practices that others were following.

However, as I opened up to these other practices, I found myself confronted with a great deal of confusion. I was uncertain about which practices to incorporate into my own path. I fell into the trap of wondering, 'Which is the right or best spiritual practice to follow on my journey?'

When I finally understood that my practices were not the ultimate truth but rather a point of reference, I felt a bit unsteady. Why? Because as humans, we are always in search of truth or the right path to follow. It left me wondering where to look for truth if my practices were not it. Which path should I follow? However, these lines showed me a completely different side of the story and resolved all my queries!

> To find the origin,
> trace back the manifestations.
>
> Use your own light
> and return to the source of light.
> This is called practicing eternity.

I pondered upon what Lao Tzu meant by the 'practice of eternity'. It was only after re-reading and reflecting on these lines repeatedly that I came to the realisation that all the practices I engaged in were merely outward expressions.

Each person adheres to a set of beliefs, practices, or a religious path. I came to the realisation that these external manifestations, or the 'children', were the aspects I was getting attached to. I understood that I needed to move beyond these manifestations and seek the mother, the source, which is, indeed, the absolute truth from which everything originated.

As I released my attachments to my practices and ceased viewing them as the ultimate truth, my heart opened up to connect with that source, the origin of everything. This source conveyed to me that all practices serve as means to reach the absolute truth where all distinctions dissolve, and unity prevails.

By utilising my own inner wisdom and returning to that source of light—the absolute truth, which permeates everything, including you and me—I came to a profound realisation: there is no single, definitive absolute truth! Every path is merely a conduit to reach the source of eternal joy and bliss. Therefore, it is perfectly fine to hold onto your chosen paths as long as they serve their purpose, but it is equally important to be prepared to let them go when the time is right.

Take Aways

The specific path you choose for your spiritual journey to connect with the source is not of paramount importance; what truly matters is you and your intention! These practices should never define you as they are merely supportive frameworks to facilitate your journey. Whenever you find that a practice is becoming burdensome, take a moment to become present, recognise it, and break free from the cycle.

When you start viewing your practices, or any path or religion you follow, as tools aimed at reaching the source, you will come to realise that everyone is on their unique path, and no path can be labelled as right or wrong, better or worse. Each of us is consciously or unconsciously striving to return to that source of bliss. You don't need to abandon your own practices to respect someone else's. You can continue to practice what resonates most with you but do so with an attitude of flexibility. This approach opens the door for us to be receptive and accepting of diverse viewpoints.

Thich Nhat Hanh, in his book, *Being Peace,* echoes a similar perspective on the practices and doctrines individuals follow in their lives:

Aware of the suffering created by fanaticism and intolerance, we are determined not to be idolatrous about or bound to any doctrine, theory, or ideology, even Buddhist ones. Buddhist teachings are guiding means to help us learn to look deeply and to develop our understanding and compassion. They are not doctrines to fight, kill, or die for.

How to Return to the Truth of 'No Absolute Truth'

1. Today, take a moment to observe instances where you are driven to uncover the 'truth'. The truth about why you fell ill or about what is hidden agenda of your colleague at work, or the truth about why someone said something to you or why something happened to you and so on. Notice your inclination to seek the truth behind various situations. Instead of fixating on the 'why' or the ultimate truth behind a circumstance, take a step back and ask yourself, 'Given my current situation, what actions should I take?' and 'What's my next move?' Then, proceed to act based on what you discern as your next steps.
2. As an additional exercise, pay attention to whether you feel tied to the routines you engage in. These routines don't have to be spiritual; they could be any daily practice, such as a sports or fitness regimen. Can you miss a

day of practice without feeling guilt or regret? This doesn't imply that you should abandon the structures that support your practice. It is an exercise to reduce your attachment to your own routines and to prevent excessive fixation. Dedicate one day a week to deliberately skip your regular practice and embrace that choice without judgement. Remember that your practices are not synonymous with your identity; they are tools for physical and mental well-being. Resume your practice the following day, engaging in what you are meant to do.

Chapter 24

The Bliss of Letting Go of Bliss

We all feel a variety of emotions in our day-to-day life. Generally, if we are progressing in life and achieving our goals, we feel positive emotions such as joy, fulfilment, excitement, and contentment. On the other hand, whenever we fail or fall in life, we tend to feel negative emotions such as sadness, frustration, disappointment, and stress. And though we all would prefer positive emotions and rather avoid negative ones, this isn't the best approach for a holistic and wholesome life. Let me share a personal experience to illustrate the same.

While practising some of the previously mentioned exercises, I took some time to reflect on what I had been doing and how I had been feeling in this whole process.

This was a time period when I was totally committed to these exercises and had been giving my hundred per cent to the process. This meant that I was regularly practising gratitude and trying to live life with no judgements or separation. I saw everyone and everything as a part of one, big whole and was compassionate to every being that

I encountered, from bees to human beings. I was now automatically living from a knowing that I was not the doer and that everything was already happening as per the divine order. To put it succinctly, I was surrendering every bit of my life to the universe, and it was responding with love and abundance.

In such a space, everything was getting done effortlessly and I felt immense fulfilment, joy, and bliss. Earlier, I used to come in and out of these experiences, but the difference this time was that I experienced them for a longer period consistently.

And as my joy and fulfilment increased, my attachment to these positive emotions also increased. Simply put, I wanted to make these positive emotions a permanent part of my life and never fall back to lower frequency states of misery, anger, and anxiety. I was desperately trying to cling to something and not let it go as I feared that if I did so, it would be lost forever.

At this point, I came across the thirty-sixth verse of the Tao Te Ching which acted as my guiding light and brought me back on track. It reads as follows:

> Should you want to contain something,
> You must deliberately let it expand.
> Should you want to weaken something,
> You must deliberately let it grow strong.
> Should you want to eliminate something,
> You must deliberately allow it to flourish.
> Should you want to take something away,

You must deliberately grant it access.

This verse really made me reconsider and reanalyse why I was doing the things I was doing. I could see that I really disliked the low states of fear, anger, and anxiety. I then asked myself the reason why I so vehemently disliked these lower states which led to an epiphany. I realised that the main reason why I avoided these lower states was because I didn't want to become like people in my life who were fearful, angry, or anxious!

When I further explored this line of questioning, I realised that it wasn't the people but their traits or the emotions they carried that made me uncomfortable. And thus, the only way I could accept other people as well as myself when such emotions showed up in me was to accept these emotions in the first place.

After this, I stopped segregating emotions into positive and negative categories. I realised that all human emotions are important and serve a unique purpose. This not only made me more accepting of other people, myself and life in general but also released me from the burden of constantly vetting emotions.

Take Aways

True freedom means not being bound by anything. But often, when we are on our journey of transformation, we develop attachments to the blissful experiences. This attachment makes us strive to somehow permanently capture these experiences and make them last forever. But the truth is that the moment we try to capture something, we lose it. And when we don't hold on to things and experiences and allow them to take their natural course, they return to us in abundance.

Therefore, it is important to constantly remind yourself to let go of everything you are trying to accumulate or are fearful of losing. The following excerpt from Sri Nisargadatta Maharaj beautifully summarises this message.

> Between the banks of pain and pleasure, the river of life flows. It is only when the mind refuses to flow with life, and gets stuck at the banks, that it becomes a problem. By flowing with life, I mean acceptance—letting come what comes and go what goes.

How to Let Go of Attachments to Positive Emotions and Experiences

If you find yourself inclining towards certain experiences while resisting others, it is very likely that you are caught in the trap of attachment. The steps given below can assist you in letting go of your attachments and accepting life in its totality.

1. Pick up your journal and note down your answers to questions such as:
    - Why do I resist lower states? Is there a deeper reason behind this resistance?
    - Why am I attached to the higher frequency states and what is the reason I am not willing to let them go?

- What will happen if I simply let go of these blissful experiences?

2. If you honestly answer these questions, you will notice that your preferences and dislikes have deeper reasons for them and once you get hold of the root cause, only then you can act upon them. And by accepting all kinds of emotions and experiences that life has to offer, including the ones that you are uncomfortable with, you will open up a new world for you.

There is an additional practice which you can try out as well. Be on the lookout for the experiences which you want to seize and make them a permanent part of your life. It could be something as simple as listening to your favourite song on repeat. But once you start listening to the same song over and over again, you will notice that your excitement and the original joy which you experienced diminishes when you listen to it for the fifth or the sixth time. Then, instead of playing your favourite song, listen to whatever song that comes up next. This might sound like a very simple practice, but it symbolises the conscious step towards letting go of the attachment to the joy you experience when your favourite song is playing. This way, whenever you next get to hear your favourite song, whether on the radio or some other place, you will find it more exciting than ever before. All in all, this mindful practice contemplation and experimentation can make you more open to other things and reinstill the things you love with more love and joy.

ACKNOWLEDGEMENTS

It has been a memorable and transformative journey that started with the inception of the book to writing it and finally, getting it published. I would like to thank all the people who pushed me forward on this journey.

First and foremost, I would like to thank Lao Tzu for writing the Tao Te Ching and sharing his immense wisdom with the world.

I am also grateful to various translators who tactfully translated the multifaceted text of The Tao Te Ching into the English language. This includes Derek Bryce and Léon Wieger, Sam Hamill, Stephen Mitchell, Gia-Fu Feng and Jane English, Stephen Hodge, Thomas Clearly, Jonathan Star, John C. H. Wu, Michael Latorra, and Witter Bynner.

I would also like to express my gratitude to Dr Wayne Dyer for arousing the spark in me to read the Tao Te Ching.

To my friend, baido, Dr Sarmishtha Sarma, for believing in this work as well as for reviewing and giving me nourishing inputs each time.

Thank you, Axaya Kansal, Priyanka Mittal, and Anna Lobanova for their refined guidance and valuable suggestions from start to end.

I would like to thank Aditya Jarial and the entire team of Hay House India Publications for believing in my work and giving me a platform to share it with the world.

The space that surrounds us contributes to the results we produce. Amsterdamse Bos was one such space that stimulated and nurtured my creativity and guided me during the writing process. I would like to thank the municipality of Amsterdam and Amstelveen for maintaining such a beautiful forest for the residents.

My deep love and gratitude to my dearest husband, my best friend, for his unconditional support and constant push to achieve my goals. Thank you for understanding me when I am not able to understand myself.

To my parents and parents-in-law for being that lovely tree under which I feel safe and loved.

To my sisters for always being there through the thick and thin. Thank you Kanupriya Beri, Shivani Dave, and Ankita Kawatra.

To Stuti Rawat for being for her unfailing love and support through it all.

Moving to a new country has been an exciting venture for me and I would like to show my gratitude to everyone who offered their friendship to me in this new country and the ones who challenged me as they were the real spiritual teachers to me, pushing me to connect with my deeper self.

Finally, I would like to thank the life force that created me and everything in this universe and without the support of which this work would have never manifested in the physical world.

References

Chapter 1: Effortless Action

Quotation 1:

For one who is happy in the Self alone, who is satisfied in the Self, who is content only in the Self, there is nothing that has to be done. [3:17]

Reference: The Bhagavad Gita.

Chapter 2: Being Nothing

Quotation 1:

You enter a world where conjuring something out of nothing is possible. That is because at this scale, particles such as protons, behave according to the laws of nature we call 'quantum mechanics', and they really can appear at random, stick around for a while, and then vanish again to reappear somewhere else.

Reference: Hawking, S. (2018). *Brief Answers to the Big Questions*. Bantam.

Quotation 2:

Wisdom is knowing I am nothing,

Love is knowing I am everything,

and between the two my life moves.

Reference: Nisargadatta, M. (2012). *I Am That: Talks with Sri Nisargadatta Maharaj*. Acorn Press.

Chapter 3: The Act of Allowing

Quotation 1:

In life, there is suffering, because of the impermanent nature of things.

Suffering is due to attachments and expectations, to grasping and clinging.

It's possible to end suffering by giving up attachments (clinging) and expectations (grasping).

The way to end suffering due to clinging and grasping is through balance and living in the present.

Reference: Alexander, R. (2009). *Wise Mind, Open Mind: Finding Purpose and Meaning in Times of Crisis, Loss, and Change.* New Harbinger Publications.

Chapter 4: Being Water

Quotation 1:

Water does not resist. Water flows. When you plunge your hand into it, all you feel is a caress. Water is not a solid wall, it will not stop you. But water always goes where it wants to go, and nothing in the end can stand against it. Water is patient. Dripping water wears away a stone. Remember that, my child. Remember you are half water. If you can't go through an obstacle, go around it. Water does.

Reference: Atwood, Margaret (2005-10-11). *The Penelopiad: Canongate Myth Series,* Toronto: Knopf Canada, ISBN 0-676-97425-2.

Chapter 6: Detachment to Success and Failure

Quotation 1:

If you take your success too seriously, you get entangled and fail to use the objects of your success as a means for the next level of achievement-the spiritual. Thus, right from the beginning of your worldly endeavours, desist from the cravings of the senses and maintain awareness that although the worldly objects provide some degree of comfort, ultimately, they are worthless.

Reference: Tigunait, P. R. (2002). *The Himalayan Masters: A Living Tradition.* Himalayan Institute Press.

Chapter 7: Being One with Everything

Quotation 1:

The Self is the essence of this universe, the essence of all souls; He is the essence of your own life, nay, 'Thou are That'. You are one with this universe. He who says he is different from others, even by a hair's breadth, immediately becomes miserable. Happiness belongs to him who knows this oneness, who knows he is one with this universe.

Reference: Bentlage, B., Eggert, M., Krämer, H. M., & Reichmuth, S. (Eds.). (2016). *Religious Dynamics under the Impact of Imperialism and Colonialism: A Sourcebook.* Brill.

Chapter 8: Communicating with Our Bodies

Quotation 1:

The body is a multilingual being. It speaks through its colour and its temperature, the flush of recognition, the glow of love, the ash of pain, the heat of arousal, the coldness of non-conviction. It speaks through its constant tiny dance, sometimes swaying, sometimes a—jitter, sometimes trembling. It speaks through the leaping of the heart, the falling of the spirit, the pit at the center, and rising hope. The body remembers, the bones remember, the joints remember, even the little finger remembers. Memory is lodged in pictures and feelings in the cells themselves. Like a sponge filled with water, anywhere the flesh is pressed, wrung, even touched lightly, a memory may flow out in a stream.

Reference: Estes, C. P. (1995). *Women Who Run with the Wolves: Myths and Stories of the Wild Woman Archetype.* Ballantine Books.

Chapter 9: Going beyond Uncertainty

Quotation 1:

Be patient toward all that is unsolved in your heart and try to love the questions themselves like locked rooms and like books that are written in a very foreign tongue. Do not now seek the answers, which cannot be given you because you would not be able to live them. And the point is, to live everything. Live the questions now. Perhaps you will then gradually, without noticing it, live along some distant day into the answer.

Reference: Rilke, R. M. (1954). *Letters to a Young Poet* (MD Herter Norton, Trans.). New York: WW. (Multiple references)

Chapter 10: Running behind the Unreal

Quotation 1:

The real does not die, the unreal never lived.

Once you know that death happens to the body and not to you, you just watch your body falling off like a discarded garment.

The real you is timeless and beyond birth and death. The body will survive as long as it needed. It is not important that it should live long.

Reference: Nisargadatta, M. (2012). *I Am That: Talks with Sri Nisargadatta Maharaj*. Acorn Press.

Chapter 11: The Art of Non-Interference

Quotation 1:
Refuse all thoughts except one: the thought 'I am'. The mind will rebel in the beginning, but with patience and perseverance it will yield and keep quiet. Once you are quiet, things will begin to happen spontaneously and quite naturally without any interference on your part.

Reference: Nisargadatta, M. (2012). *I Am That: Talks with Sri Nisargadatta Maharaj*. Acorn Press.

Chapter 12: Transcending Morality and Ethics

Quotation 1:
In its goal of radical self-transcendence, Yoga even intends to reach beyond the level of normative behaviour or learned morality. In order to live authentically, the sages insist, we must transcend the human-made categories of 'good' and 'evil', which vary from culture to culture, even sometimes from group to group.

Reference: Feuerstein, G. (2007). *Yoga Morality: Ancient Teachings at a Time of Global Crisis.* Hohm Press.

Chapter 13: Loving the Enemy

Quotation 1:
If I want to be loved as I am,
I have to be willing to love others as they are.

Reference: Louise Hay, *Dissolving Barriers: Discover Your Subconscious Blocks to Love, Health and a Powerful Self-Image.*

Chapter 14: Nurturing Humility

Quotation 1:

Humility, pridelessness, nonviolence, tolerance, simplicity, approaching a bona fide spiritual master, cleanliness, steadiness and self-control; renunciation of the objects of sense gratification, absence of false ego, the perception of the evil of birth, death, old age and disease; nonattachment to children, wife, home and the rest, and even mindedness amid pleasant and unpleasant events; constant and unalloyed devotion to Me, resorting to solitary places, detachment from the general mass of people; accepting the importance of self-realisation, and philosophical search for the Absolute Truth-all these I thus declare to be knowledge, and what is contrary to these is ignorance.

Reference: The Bhagavad Gita.

Chapter 15: Slowing Down

Quotation 1:

It does not matter how much time we are given if there is nowhere for it to settle; it escapes through the cracks and holes of the mind.

Reference: *On the Shortness of Life: Life Is Long if You Know How to Use It* (Penguin Great Ideas) by Seneca (Author), C. D. N. Costa (Translator).

Chapter 16: Breaking Your Bondage

Quotation 1:

First destroy the mental conditioning by renouncing cravings; and then remove from your mind even the concept of bondage and liberation. Be totally free of conditioning. Ideas and thoughts are bondage; and their coming to an end is liberation. Therefore, be free of them and do whatever has to be done spontaneously.

Reference: Venkatesananda, S. (2010). *Vasistha's Yoga.* SUNY Press.

Chapter 17: Forests—My Eternal Partner

Quotation 1:
Look deep into the nature, and
then you will understand everything better.

Reference: Quote to Margot Einstein, after his sister's (Maja) death, 1951; quote by Hanna Loewy in A&E Television Einstein Biography, VPI International, 1991.**

Chapter 18: Clarity amidst Chaos

Quotation 1:
They in whom the spirit of inquiry is ever awake illumine the world, enlighten all who come into contact with them, dispel the ghosts created by an ignorant mind, and realize the falsity of sense-pleasures and their objects. O Rama, in the light of inquiry there is realisation of the eternal and unchanging reality; this is the supreme. With it one does not long for any other gain nor does one spurn anything. He is free from delusion, attachment; he is not inactive nor does he get drowned in action; he lives and functions in this world and at the end of a natural life-span he reaches the blissful state of total freedom. The eye of spiritual inquiry does not lose its sight even in the midst of all activities.

Reference: Chapple, C. K. (2010). *The Concise Yoga Vasistha.* SUNY Press.

Quotation 2:
When the mind is disturbed by improper thoughts, constant pondering over the opposites is the remedy.

Reference: Taimni, I. K. (1961). *The Science of Yoga*. Quest Books.

Chapter 19: Accepting All of Me

Quotation 1:
Understanding is love,
If you can't understand, you cannot love.
When you understand yourself, you love yourself.

Reference: Thich Nhat Hanh**

Chapter 21: Embracing Death

Quotation 1:
This body is not me; I am not caught in this body, I am life without boundaries, I have never been born and I have never died. Over there the wide ocean and the sky with many galaxies; All manifests from the basis of consciousness. Since beginningless time I have always been free
Birth and death are only a door through which we go in and out. Birth and death are only a game of hide-and-seek. So smile to me and take my hand and wave good-bye. Tomorrow we shall meet again or even before. We shall always be meeting again at the true source, Always meeting again on the myriad paths of life.

Reference: Hanh, T. N. (2003). *No Death, No Fear: Comforting Wisdom for Life*. Penguin.

Chapter 22: Choice—The Source of Confusion

Quotation 1:

If you obsess over whether you are making the right decision, you are basically assuming that the universe will reward you for one thing and punish you for another. The universe has no fixed agenda. Once you make any decision, it works around that decision. There is no right or wrong, only a series of possibilities that shift with each thought, feeling, and action that you experience. If this sounds too mystical, refer again to the body. Every significant vital sign- body temperature, heart rate, oxygen consumption, hormone level, brain activity, and so on- alters the moment you decide to do anything . . . decisions are signals telling your body, mind, and environment to move in a certain direction.

Reference: Lord, D. C. (2004). *The Book of Secrets: Unlocking the Hidden Dimensions of Your Life.*

Chapter 23: The Absolute Truth

Quotation 1:

Aware of the suffering created by fanaticism and intolerance, we are determined not to be idolatrous about or bound to any doctrine, theory, or ideology, even Buddhist ones. Buddhist teachings are guiding means to help us learn to look deeply and to develop our understanding and compassion. They are not doctrines to fight, kill, or die for.

Reference: Hanh, T. N. (2020). *Being Peace.* Parallax Press.

Chapter 24: The Bliss of Letting Go of Bliss

Quotation 1:

Between the banks of pain and pleasure, the river of life flows. It is only when the mind refuses to flow with life, and gets stuck at the banks, that it becomes a problem. By flowing with life, I mean acceptance—letting come what comes and go what goes.

Reference: Nisargadatta, M. (2012). *I Am That: Talks with Sri Nisargadatta Maharaj.* Acorn Press.